SUPER-SCARY
SCARY
MOCHIMOCHI

SUPER-SCARY

20+ CUTE & CREEPY CREATURES TO KNIT

MOCHIMOCHI

ANNA HRACHOVEC

Photographs by Brandi Simons

POTTER CRAFT

New York

Copyright © 2012 by Anna Hrachovec

All rights reserved.
Published in the United States by Potter Craft, an imprint of
the Crown Publishing Group, a division of Random House,
Inc., New York.
www.pottercraft.com
www.crownpublishing.com

POTTER CRAFT and colophon is a registered trademark of
Random House, Inc.

Library of Congress Cataloging-in-Publication Data
Hrachovec, Anna
Super-scary mochimochi: 20+ cute and creepy creatures to
knit /
Anna Hrachovec; photography by Brandi Simons. — 1st
edition
pages cm.
Includes index.
I. Amigurumi—Patterns. 2. Soft toy making. I. Simons, Brandi,
illustrator. II. Title.
TT829.H733 2011
745.592'4—dc23   2011046773

ISBN 978-0-307-96576-9
eISBN 978-0-307-96577-6

Printed in China

Design by Laura Palese
Cover photographs by Brandi Simons

Photographs on the following pages copyright © 2012 by
Brandi Simons: 2, 4, 8, 17, 38, 43, 45, 48, 52, 60–61, 66, 69,
70, 74, 79, 80, 88, 90, 92, 95, 100–101, 102, 105, 107, 112, 117,
118, 122, 127, 130–131

Photograph on page 73 copyright © 2012 by Jenna Leigh Teti

All other photographs copyright © 2012 by Anna Hrachovec

The author and publisher would like to thank the Craft Yarn
Council of America for providing the yarn weight standards
and accompanying icons used in this book. For more
information, please visit www.YarnStandards.com.

10 9 8 7 6 5 4 3 2 1

First Edition

FOR NORA!

....

ACKNOWLEDGMENTS

Thank you to John, always my cheerleader and my first consultant on design and the written word. Many, many thanks to Brandi for her gung-ho spirit, endless creativity, and talent with a camera. The whole Simons family—Mike, Sonnie, and Sarah—deserves lots of ice cream for their hours of help and patient modeling. Another big thank-you to my sister-in-law, Jenna, for her photography session with my two drowsy cats.

Thank you to Robert Sheaff at the University of Tulsa and Jeremy Hopkins at Modern Day Dentil in Owasso for their generosity with space and equipment that is normally used for much more important tasks.

My thanks to Audrey for her help with brainstorming weird monsters, and to Angela for her advice about lacemaking and also her testing help. As always, my parents and sister, Leah, supplied ideas and multiple props, even if they weren't aware of it because they were on vacation at the time.

I cannot thank my testers enough for making the patterns in this book user friendly. Many thanks to my mother-in-law, Bonney, and to Denise, Jennifer, Jenny, Jessica, Joan, Kari, Kelly, Kristen, Lisa, Marilyn, Mary, Marti, and Rikke.

Thank you to Shannon and Stacy at Cascade Yarns for supplying the beautiful yarn used in every project in this book.

I am extremely grateful to Joy Aquilino for her concept and initiation of the publication process. Thank you to my editor, Betty Wong, and to Caitlin Harpin for diligently seeing the book through its publication journey. Many thanks to Linda Hetzer for her careful and always thoughtful editing. I am also very thankful for the support and enthusiasm of Kimberly Small and everyone else at Potter Craft.

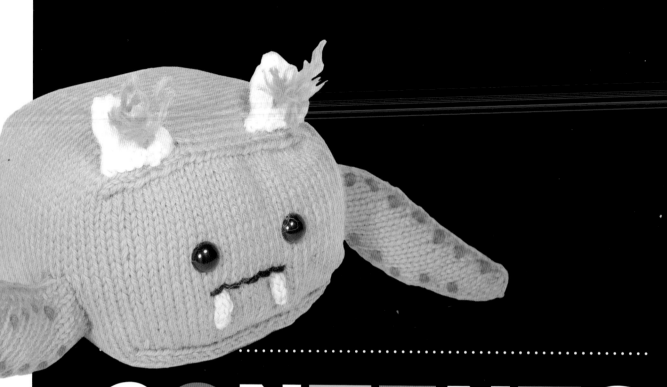

CONTENTS

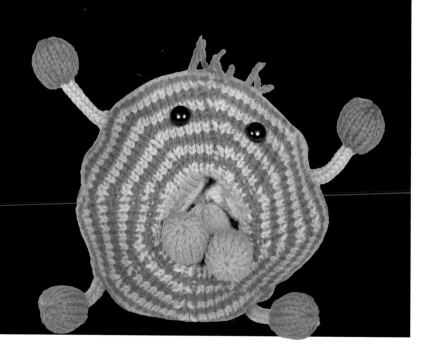

INTRODUCTION: BOO! 9
ENTER IF YOU DARE . . . 10

OLD-SCHOOL GHOULS
36

BACK-YARD BEASTIES
64

CREEPY NEW SPECIES
86

MIX 'N' MATCH MONSTERS
110

BOO!

Did I scare you? Yeah, I didn't think so. I've been working really hard on my big, scary font and everything, but I still haven't gotten it down yet. Oh, well. I've come to accept that I'm a very unintimidating knitter of toys, but the fibrous monsters, beasts, and ghoulies that lurk in these pages are under the impression that they're all really scary. Like, SUPER-SCARY. In reality, they couldn't even scare my cat, and he gets spooked if you sneeze. I like to think the creatures that inhabit this book are more cute than scary, though I would never say that to their faces.

You see, under all that ego, the mochis in SUPER-SCARY MOCHIMOCHI have a sensitive side, so do me a favor and indulge them just a little. Give them your best horror-movie scream when you turn the page, would you?

Other than some emotional reassurance, what do these adorable abominations want from you? They want you to confront your fears by re-creating them for yourself, of course! The projects in this book will have you knitting some of the oddest toys you've ever seen, from teensy-weensy zombies to a big tooth-eating tooth, and you can even dream up your own creepy concoctions with the Mix 'n Match Monsters chapter. Make them for anybody who could use a good scream or a good laugh. Silly scary stuff has no age limits!

With a little innovation, your version might even be a little scarier than the originals. And, if you think about it, what's more dangerous than a clever knitter wielding yarn and needles? So with this guide in hand, go forth and knit up some creatures that will go bump in the night, eat your iPad alive, or just stare back at you in a deeply unsettling way.

ENTER IF YOU DARE

Knitters, are you prepared to release your inner Dr. Frankenstein? To set loose on the world toys that only a madman could love? If so, the right book for you is now in your clutches.

WEAPONS INVENTORY

Knitting a toy is not as scary as it looks—as long as you don't feel queasy at the sight of pointy needles, stitchy seams, and fluffy guts. But beware! You're about to become prisoner to a new knitting addiction. There's no turning back now, so it's time to familiarize yourself with the raw materials you'll be working with.

YARN

Monster-y mochis can be made out of all kinds of yarn: thin, thick, wooly, or synthetic. Combining different colors and textures is part of the fun of knitting toys, which give you great freedom to experiment.

Most of the toys in this book are made with wool yarn in three different weights, depending on the project: fingering (thin yarn suitable for tiny knits and small details), worsted (a medium-weight yarn used for many types of knits), and bulky (a still-thicker yarn that knits up quickly).

Yarn is made from a wide variety of materials. All can be used for knitting toys, although there are differences in how different fibers look, feel, and wear over time. Here are some common fibers.

WOOL I like to knit with wool because of its soft, flexible feel. There are many different blends and varieties of wool yarn available; wool blended with synthetic fibers and superwash wools are easier to wash than all wool.

COTTON Another natural fiber, cotton is durable and beautiful. It's generally not as easy to work with or as forgiving as wool, but it's a good choice when knitting for small children or people who are allergic to wool.

ACRYLIC A great choice for many toy knitters, acrylic is affordable, durable, and washable. It is less flexible than wool, and some knitters avoid it because it's not a natural fiber.

OTHER FIBERS AND BLENDS There are many yarns available in other fibers, both natural and synthetic, so you can experiment with them. An unconventional or novelty yarn may be a tricky choice for a big sweater project, but for a silly scary toy, it might be just the thing.

Most of the projects in this book use less than one skein of each color of yarn recommended, and many use only small amounts of any given color. So I suggest checking your stash first to see if you have enough scrap yarn on hand. If you buy full skeins of yarn to make a toy, you might just have enough yarn to make multiples.

NEEDLES

DOUBLE-POINTED NEEDLES Double-pointed needles (DPNs, for short) are often the best choice when knitting toys because they allow you to knit in the round in varying circumference sizes. DPNs come in sets of five, although you will usually work with only four needles at a time—three needles to hold your stitches, and a fourth needle to knit with.

CIRCULAR NEEDLE A circular needle is great for knitting in the round, especially for pieces with larger circumferences. I recommend using a circular needle for some of the patterns in this book, although you can always use DPNs instead. You can also do small-circumference circular knitting with a long circular needle, using a technique called magic loop knitting. (See Magic Loop Knitting on page 34.) This is a good choice for people who are not so comfortable with DPNs.

STRAIGHT NEEDLES Straight needles are the standard choice for knitting flat pieces. However, both DPNs and circular needles can do double duty for working flat pieces, so I rarely use straight needles.

YARN WEIGHT SYSTEM   Adapted from the Standard Yarn Weight System of the Craft Yarn Council of America

YARN WEIGHT CATEGORIES	TYPES OF YARN IN CATEGORY	KNIT GAUGE RANGE (IN STOCKINETTE STITCH TO 4")	RECOMMENDED NEEDLE SIZES (US/METRIC SIZES)
0 LACE	Fingering, 10-count crochet thread	33–40 sts	000–1/1.5–2.25mm
1 SUPER FINE	Sock, fingering, baby	27–32 sts	1–3/2.25–3.25mm
2 FINE	Sport, baby	23–26 sts	3–5/3.25–3.75mm
3 LIGHT	DK, light worsted	21–24 sts	5–7/3.75–4.5mm
4 MEDIUM	Worsted, afghan, aran	16–20 sts	7–9/4.5–5.5mm
5 BULKY	Chunky, craft, rug	12–15 sts	9–11/5.5–8mm
6 SUPER BULKY	Bulky, roving	6–11 sts	11 and larger/8mm and larger

When choosing the size of needles to use, keep in mind that your stitches should be tighter when knitting toys than they need to be when knitting a garment. This is so that the stuffing doesn't show through in the finished toy. As a general rule, you can go down two or three sizes from the size typically recommended on the label for the type of yarn you're working with. (See the Yarn Weight System chart on page 13.)

Another way to choose the right needle size for a project is to check your gauge against the gauge noted in a pattern. (See Monstersizing on page 16.)

When deciding what length needles to use, consider how big or small the circumference of your knitting will be for your project. If you will be knitting a very small toy (with 40 stitches or less, for example), shorter needles will be less cumbersome to use. For larger toys, longer needles are more suitable. In the patterns in this book, needle length is noted when it's important to the project.

Needles come in a variety of materials, including wood, bamboo, metal, and plastic. Many local craft stores will let you try out different needles before buying, so you can find which ones you're most comfortable with. My personal preference is bamboo or wood DPNs and metal circular needles.

STUFFING

Like yarn and needles, stuffing comes in a variety of materials: wool, bamboo, and my preferred material, polyester. Each one has a different weight and texture; for example, wool is denser and gives a toy a nice, heavy weight, while polyester is springy and light.

Some of the toy patterns require you to weave I-cord pieces through a stuffed body and polyester stuffing is a good choice because it is less likely to grab onto the knitted piece as it passes through. Polyester is also the best choice for toys that will be washed, because it dries quickly and is less likely to become moldy.

In a pinch, especially for small projects, you can stuff your toy with scraps of yarn.

EYES

Eyes can be made of yarn, beads, buttons, or a variety of other materials. Use your imagination, especially when making silly monsters!

I use plastic "safety eyes" in most of the projects in this book. They're easy to use, snap in place, and stay put. Despite the name, they're not safe for children under the age of three. A simple kid-safe alternative is to embroider eyes using a contrasting-colored yarn. (See Knitting for Little Ghouls on page 16.)

TOOLS

SCISSORS Scissors are a must, and a pair with a pointed tip is best to use with knitting projects.

TAPESTRY NEEDLE Like a jumbo-sized sewing needle, a tapestry needle is used with yarn for seaming, embroidering details, and weaving in loose ends. Some varieties have a bent tip, which makes it easier to go in and out of a knitted piece.

STITCH MARKER Stitch markers help you remember where the rounds in your knitting begin and end. You can buy small plastic rings, or you can simply tie a small piece of contrasting-colored yarn in a loop.

CROCHET HOOK A crochet hook is useful for making a provisional cast-on, for attaching hair to a toy, or for picking up stitches dropped accidentally. Use one that's approximately the same size as the knitting needles you are using.

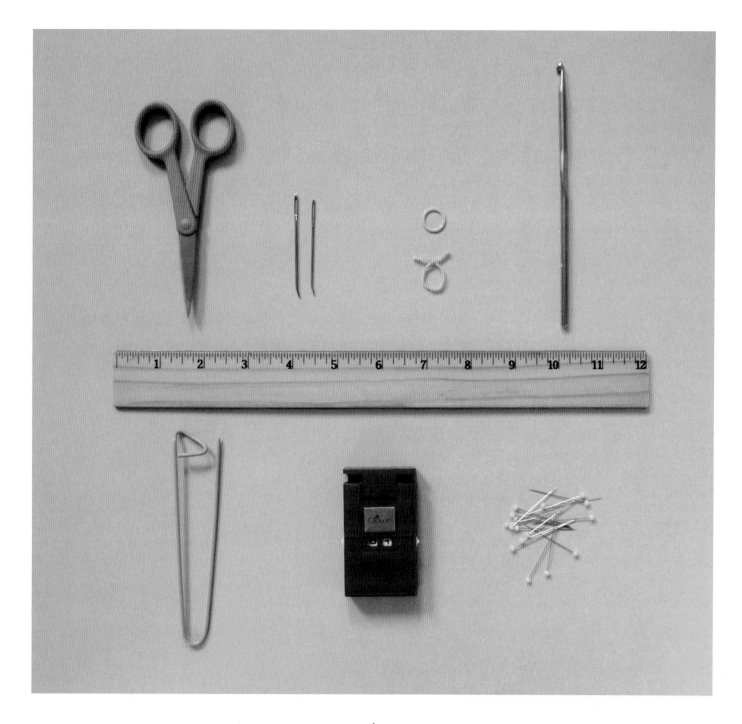

STITCH COUNTER A stitch counter helps you keep track of the row or round you're on; the type pictured is an easy-to-use clicking device. Or you can simply make hash marks on a piece of paper.

STITCH HOLDER Like a large safety pin, a stitch holder allows you to hold live stitches temporarily so that you can come back to them later. You can also use a spare needle in lieu of a holder, or simply thread a piece of waste yarn through the live stitches and tie it closed.

TAPE MEASURE OR RULER This is essential for checking gauge or for a wearable project that needs to be measured.

STRAIGHT PINS Straight pins are helpful when you're attaching pieces together so you can get the spacing right before you sew them in place.

KNITTING FOR LITTLE GHOULS

If your scary mochi will end up in the paws of a child aged three or younger, make sure the toy is age-appropriate before you begin to knit.

- Use medium- or bulky-weight yarn for small toys so they are at least 2" (5cm) in diameter in every direction (and not a choking hazard).
- Embroider eyes with a contrasting-colored yarn. Plastic eyes, although commonly called "safety eyes," are not safe for small kids.
- Make seams extra secure by sewing around them twice and weave loose ends through the toy multiple times.

MONSTERSIZING

Checking gauge is the best way to make sure that your finished project will be the same size as the sample shown in the book. That said, the only time that it's really important to match gauge is when size is essential, as in a wearable garment or an iPad case (hello, Flatso!).

If you choose not to check gauge, all you need to do is keep in mind that your stitches should be tight enough that stuffing won't show through the knitted fabric in your finished toy. If you are a loose knitter, you may need to go one size down from the recommended needle size in the pattern (which is already two or three sizes smaller than would be typically recommended for the yarn used in the project).

Checking gauge takes only a few minutes and a few simple steps:

1. Using the yarn you have chosen for a project and the needle size called for in the pattern, knit a flat square about 5" by 5" (12.5cm x 12.5cm) in stockinette stitch (knit on the right side, purl on the wrong side).

2. Lay the square flat without stretching it—it's helpful to pin it to an ironing board or another surface so it won't slip around—and use a ruler or tape measure to measure how many stitches and how many rows you have per inch.

3. If your stitch/row counts are significantly smaller than in the given gauge (i.e., your knitting is looser than in the sample), switch to a smaller-sized needle and try again. If your stitch/row counts are significantly larger than in the given gauge (i.e., your knitting is tighter than in the sample), you can try using a larger-sized needle. However, if using a larger needle makes gaps between your stitches, then try using a thicker yarn instead.

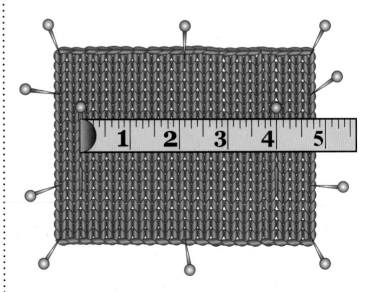

THE GORY DETAILS

If you know the basics of knitting, but you're new to knitting toys, this section will get you started. For knitting basics and general techniques, refer to Knitting Essentials on page 132.

USING DOUBLE-POINTED NEEDLES

Knitting in the round is a great way to make three-dimensional toys with minimal seaming, and I prefer to use double-pointed needles (DPNs) when knitting most toys. (For using a circular needle, see Magic Loop Knitting on page 34.)

DPNs look much scarier than they are. The trick is to focus on the two needles that you're currently using, and let the other needles hold your other stitches until you come around to them.

1. Begin by using just one needle to cast on all your stitches. Then, distribute the stitches onto three needles, slipping them purlwise onto the new needles. (If you're working with a large number of stitches, you can place your stitches onto four needles and knit with the fifth needle.) Hold the needle with the attached yarn in your right hand. To make sure that you aren't twisting the stitches, align the cast-on edge to the insides of the needles.

2. If you are using a stitch marker to keep track of the beginning of your rounds, slip the marker onto the needle in your right hand, and knit the first stitch from the left needle onto the right. (If you're beginning with a very small number of stitches [see Beginning with a Small Number of Stitches, page 19], you can do this step at the beginning of a subsequent round, after you've increased your total number of stitches.)

3. Now use a fourth needle to knit the stitches on the needle in your left hand.

4. When you finish knitting from the needle in your left hand, the stitches will all end up on the right-hand needle. Slide these stitches down a bit on the right-hand needle so that they won't slip off. Then continue knitting the stitches from the next needle to the left onto your now-empty needle.

5. Sometimes, a column of loose stitches can form because of the gaps between the needles (often called the "ladder" effect). To avoid this, you can keep your tension even by shifting the stitches around the needles every few rounds. Do this by setting aside the fourth needle and knitting two stitches directly from one needle to another.

6. Continue knitting from the needle in your left hand to the needle in your right, around and around, slipping the stitch marker along when you come to it. (Every time you come to the marker, you will have just finished one round of knitting.) After knitting a few rounds, you will see a three-dimensional shape begin to form.

BEGINNING WITH A SMALL NUMBER OF STITCHES

Many of the patterns in this book begin with six or fewer stitches on the needles, and then increase that number in the first round. An easy way to start out with a small number of stitches is to begin by knitting the first round as you would an I-cord.

1. After casting on, leave your stitches on just one DPN, and slide the end that doesn't have the yarn attached to the right end of the needle.

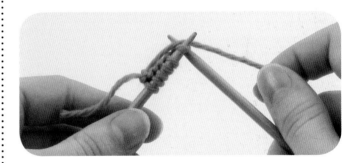

2. Bring the attached yarn around the back and, pulling tightly on the yarn, knit onto a second needle. (In most patterns, you will work a kfb increase with this stitch.)

3. Once you have finished knitting the stitches on the needle and have increased the total number of stitches, distribute the stitches onto three DPNs and continue knitting in the round.

STUFFING AND CLOSING UP

Before you close up a piece, you will usually need to stuff it. Then you will break the yarn and draw it tightly through the live stitches to finish off.

1. First, stuff the piece. This is usually done a few rounds before the end of the piece, when the opening is still big enough to poke the stuffing inside with your fingers. If you need to stuff a narrow piece, carefully use the tip of a closed pair of scissors to get the stuffing into tight places.

2. When you are finished knitting and are ready to close up the piece, cut the yarn, leaving a tail of a few inches (several cm), and thread the end onto a tapestry needle. Beginning with the first stitch in the round, thread the tapestry needle purlwise through each of the stitches in order in the round, slipping the stitches off the needles as you go.

3. Pull the end of the cut yarn tightly to draw the stitches closed.

4. To secure, thread the loose end of yarn down through the hole that you just closed up, and weave it through the piece.

ATTACHING EYES

Your toy will really come to life when you give it eyes. I have two favorite ways to add eyes to a toy.

PLASTIC SAFETY EYES Safety eyes come with a backing that snaps in place to hold the eyes securely. Despite their name, safety eyes can be pulled out between stitches, and so they should not be used in toys for kids ages three and younger.

You will need to insert the back of the eyes on the wrong side of your knitting, so you'll attach these eyes before you close up your toy's body.

After you've stuffed the body, insert the front halves of the eyes where you would like them on the toy. Be sure that you're happy with the placement—once you've attached the backing, there is no separating it from the front.

When attaching the eyes, the flatter side of the backing is placed up against the back of the black eyeball. Reach inside the toy to snap the backs in place.

EMBROIDERED EYES Another simple way to add eyes is to embroider them on with yarn and a tapestry needle. You can do this after the toy is finished and sewn up.

Locate where you would like to place the eye, and decide how big you would like your eye to be. For a medium-sized eye, you might make a horizontal stitch that spans the width of 2½ knitted stitches. For smaller eyes, the stitch may only span ½ (or one "leg") of a knitted stitch.

1. Thread a piece of contrasting-color yarn onto the tapestry needle. Insert the needle in the back of the body, and bring it out where you want to begin the eye. Because this yarn will stay in place with the stitches you make, don't worry about securing it with a knot.

2. Insert the needle 2½ stitches, or 5 stitch legs, to the right, and bring it out again in the same place where you started.

3. Make 3 or 4 more stitches this way, stitching over the same place.

Once you are happy with the shape of the eye, bring your needle out where you want to begin the second eye, and repeat the above technique.

I-CORD APPENDAGES

A simple way to make appendages, especially those that are thin and long, is to make one long I-cord that can become two arms or legs by inserting it through the body and letting both ends stick out.

1. After you finish making the I-cord as the pattern instructs, thread the tail end you used to close off the final stitches onto a tapestry needle.

2. Insert the needle into the body piece where you want one arm or leg to be, and bring the needle out at the point at which you want the other appendage to be attached. Make sure the needle is going in and out between knitted stitches, not splitting the yarn.

3. Pull the I-cord through the body, so that an equal length sticks out on each side. If you have some difficulty getting the I-cord to come out the other side, this means either that it is getting caught in the stuffing or that you split the yarn on the body with the needle and you are trying to pull the I-cord through a strand of yarn. Pull the needle out and try again.

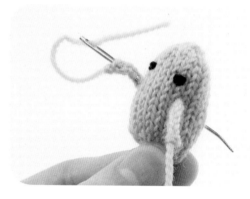

4. Once you are happy with the placement and lengths of the appendages, weave in the ends of the I-cord. Insert the tapestry needle back into the I-cord, and weave it through the I-cord and through the body. Because the I-cord is very skinny, you may need to go in and out of it a few times with the needle, but these stitches will be invisible, so don't worry about making this perfect.

5. These I-cord appendages are very poseable as you weave in the ends, so if you want your little guy to have his arms pointing up or down or sideways, now is your chance!

SEAMING

MATTRESS STITCH

Because they are worked in the round, most of the patterns in this book require minimal seaming, but when you do need to stitch parts together, beautiful seaming is easy with mattress stitch.

Mattress stitch is a technique that allows you to sew pieces together on the right sides for an almost invisible seam. There are a few variations on the simple technique, but once you understand the basics you'll see how they can be combined for all sorts of seaming. To make it easy to understand, it is shown here with flat pieces and contrasting-colored yarn.

VERTICAL MATTRESS STITCH Use this variation when you are seaming two pieces together with the vertical rows of stitches lining up.

1. On one piece, locate the first stitch on the edge of the piece, and slip the tapestry needle under the horizontal bar that appears between this stitch and the next one in from the edge. Pull the yarn through. Slip the needle under the corresponding bar on the second piece.

2. Go back to the first piece, and slip the needle under the next bar up. Go back and forth in this way a few times.

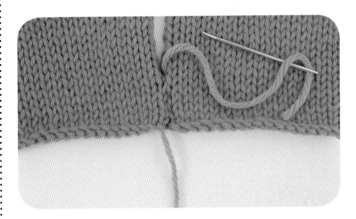

3. When you pull the yarn tightly, the seam will disappear. Continue stitching the rest of the seam.

HORIZONTAL MATTRESS STITCH Use this variation when you are seaming cast-on or bound-off edges together, or whenever two horizontal rows of stitches line up.

1. Slip the needle under the point of the V on the first stitch on the edge of one piece, and pull the yarn through. Slip the needle under the point of the corresponding V on the other piece.

2. Go back and forth in this way along the seam.

3. Pull the yarn tightly and the seam will disappear.

HORIZONTAL-TO-VERTICAL MATTRESS STITCH To seam together two pieces whose stitches run in opposite directions, you will combine the vertical and horizontal mattress stitch.

1. Slip the needle under the bar on the vertical piece and under the V on the horizontal piece. Continue to go back and forth in this way along the seam.

2. Because knitted stitches are slightly wider than they are tall, your total number of bars and Vs won't match up exactly. Compensate for this difference by slipping the needle under two bars instead of just one every few stitches.

PERPENDICULAR MATTRESS STITCH Most of the seaming for the projects in this book will be attaching three-dimensional pieces together, rather than flat pieces. On these occasions, use a combination of the previous techniques for perpendicular mattress stitch.

1. To attach two three-dimensional pieces together, locate the place where you want them to be joined, and pin or hold in place.

2. Note that at the top and bottom, the stitches on the smaller piece line up horizontally with the stitches on the larger piece. Beginning at the top, use horizontal mattress stitch until the stitches no longer line up.

3. For the next stitch on the larger piece, slip the needle diagonally down through the side of one knitted stitch and up through the middle of the stitch below it and to the left.

4. Now switch to vertical-to-horizontal mattress stitch, slipping the needle under the bars on the larger body piece and the Vs on the smaller piece.

5. When the stitches stop lining up vertical-to-horizontal, again make one or more diagonal stitches on the larger piece, then switch back to horizontal mattress stitch for the bottom of the smaller piece. Continue to seam in a circle in this way until you come back to the place where you started. The result is a seamless joining, with the smaller piece sticking straight out from the larger one.

BACKSTITCH

Backstitch is another seaming technique that you can use to attach a flat piece to a three-dimensional piece. This simple stitching technique creates a secure seam.

1. Overlap the two pieces you want to attach. Insert the tapestry needle straight down through both pieces, and bring it back up some distance away. Make the stitches the same length on top and underneath.

2. Insert the needle back down in the same place that you inserted it in Step 1, so that the second stitch abuts the first. Again, bring the needle back up at a distance equal to the length of one stitch.

3. Repeat Step 2 across the seam, then weave the loose ends down through the pieces to secure.

WHIPSTITCH

Whipstitch is an easy, very visible seaming technique. I don't use it often, but if you're going for a "stitched-together" look in your monster knits, it might be just the thing.

1. Bring the tapestry needle out next to the area to seam on the first piece. Next, insert it into the second piece—the placement can vary, if you are going for a haphazard effect—and bring the needle back out from the first piece.

2. Continue along the seam, each time inserting the needle into the second piece and bringing it up through the first piece. Then weave the loose ends through the main piece to secure.

WEAVING IN LOOSE ENDS

After knitting, stuffing, and seaming, your toy will probably have more than one loose end of yarn sticking out. What a fright!

1. Thread the loose end onto a tapestry needle.

2. Insert the needle back through the toy and bring it all the way out the other side. Weave the end in and out of the toy several times, being careful not to pull it too tightly.

3. When the end is sufficiently woven in, cut the yarn short, pressing on the toy gently so that the end will be hidden inside the toy.

SECRETS FROM THE TOY-KNITTING GRAVE

If you've made it this far, you now have one foot in the nether-world of knitting toys. Why not become scary-skilled with these extra tips and tricks for monster mochi making?

JOINING AND SEPARATING A ROUND

A handy way to make pairs of appendages, such as feet, ears, and other features, is to integrate them into one piece with a body for a seamless transition.

JOINING PIECES This technique is usually used to make feet, but can also be used to join together ears, arms, or other features that you want placed side by side.

Let's say you just finished making two feet. One foot will have the ball of yarn attached to it (Foot 1, in blue) and the other will have a loose tail of yarn (Foot 2, in pink). (The different colors are to help tell the two feet apart.)

1. Divide the stitches of each foot onto two needles, with the same number of stitches on each needle. Place Foot 1 on the right, with the working yarn on the rightmost stitch on the back needle. Place Foot 2 on the left, with the cut yarn on the rightmost stitch on the back needle.

2. While maintaining the order of the stitches, place the stitches on the front two needles together onto one needle, and the stitches on the back two needles together onto another needle. Hold the needles parallel to each other.

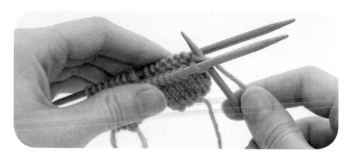

3. Pick up a third needle to knit with, and using the working yarn from the back needle, knit the stitches on the front needle.

4. When you have finished knitting the stitches on the front needle, flip the two needles around, and continue knitting the stitches on the back needle. (When you come to the loose end on the back needle, wrap it once around the working yarn to secure.)

5. When you have finished with the back needle, you have completed one round. Redistribute the stitches in order onto three needles, and pick up a fourth needle to continue knitting in a round.

SEPARATING PIECES To make seamless ears (or other appendages) at the top of your toy, you can use a technique that is basically the opposite of joining feet—separating one round of knitting into two rounds.

You will start with a round of stitches that you have worked—for ears, this will be the top of a body section that you just finished.

1. Divide the stitches onto four needles, with the same number of stitches on each needle. For example, if you have 32 stitches in your row, place 8 stitches on each needle.

2. On the next round, knit the first needle of stitches. (The contrasting-color yarn in the photos is for clarity.) Then, place the stitches from the next two needles onto a stitch holder or spare needle to work later. There should be 16 stitches on the holder.

3. Knit the stitches on the last needle, pulling the yarn tightly across the space where the stitches are held. It helps to bunch up your held stitches onto one corner of the holder.

4. Divide the 16 working stitches onto three needles, and continue to work these stitches as indicated in the pattern.

5. When you have finished the first ear, break the yarn and draw the loose end through the stitches. For the second ear, place the stitches from the holder onto three needles, and attach the yarn to the rightmost stitch on the purl side by weaving in the end with a tapestry needle.

6. Join in a round with the first stitch after the gap, and continue to work these stitches as indicated in the pattern to form the second ear.

REATTACHING YARN TO LIVE STITCHES

When you need to attach a new piece of yarn, you can usually tie it to the end of the piece you have been working with and just keep knitting. In some cases, however, you need to reattach yarn to a live stitch without the help of another piece of yarn.

1. Thread the end of the yarn onto a tapestry needle, and slip the needle through a stitch next to the first stitch that you will knit with the new yarn. Bring the needle out on the back, or purl, side of the piece, then weave the loose end through a couple of stitches on the back of the piece.

2. Loop the end of the yarn through itself to secure it.

PICKING UP STITCHES ON A THREE-DIMENSIONAL PIECE

Another seamless way to add appendages or other features to a body is to pick up stitches on the body and knit outward. This technique is ideal for small or thin appendages.

1. Decide where on the piece (usually a body) you want to pick up stitches. Depending on the placement of the stitches, you may need to turn the body sideways or upside down. Beginning with the rightmost stitch, slip the tip of a double-pointed needle under the bar between knitted stitches on the body and place the yarn between the tip of the needle and the body, with the loose end on the right.

2. With the needle, pull the yarn from under the bar, creating a loop, as you would for a standard knit stitch.

3. For subsequent stitches, repeat Steps 1 and 2 with the bar immediately to the left on the body.

TIPS ON PICKING UP STITCHES

You will always pick up stitches from right to left. This means that when you are making symmetrical appendages, you will begin picking up from opposite directions.

When picking up stitches for a left ear, begin near the top of the head and work your way down the side of the head.

When picking up stitches for a right ear, begin at the side of the head and work your way toward the top of the head.

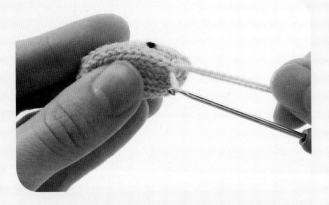

If you find it difficult to pick up the stitches by wrapping a needle, use a small crochet hook to pick up each stitch, and then slip the stitch onto a knitting needle.

EMBROIDERY

You can add a lot of personality (not to mention blood, scars, and other scary details) with some simple embroidery in a contrasting-colored yarn.

BACKSTITCH

In embroidery, backstitch is the best way to create a line on a single layer of your knitting, whether a curved or a straight line. Lines can be mouths, eyebrows, or other details.

1. Start by making your first stitch, and bring the needle out where you want the second stitch to end.

2. Pull the yarn through, then insert the needle in the same place that you inserted it for the first stitch.

3. After repeating Steps 1 and 2 several times, you will have a line of stitches that lie right next to one another with no gaps between them. For a line that curves up or down, always remember to bring your needle out where you want your next stitch to end.

DUPLICATE STITCH

Duplicate stitch is a handy technique that gives the illusion of a change in color within the knitted fabric without having to actually work the new color into the knitting.

1. Bring the needle out from the middle of a stitch, just under the downward point of the stitch's V. Then insert your needle under the V immediately above.

2. Insert the needle back down in the same place that you started to form one stitch. To make another duplicate stitch above the one you just made, bring the needle back out immediately above the place where you inserted it.

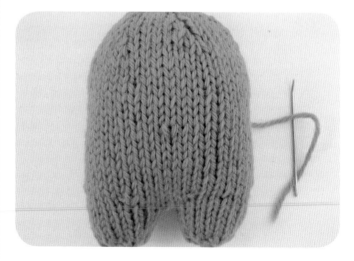

3. The result is a stitch that "duplicates" the knitted stitch beneath it in a new color. Repeat Steps 1 and 2 for each stitch.

USING A CROCHET HOOK TO ATTACH HAIR

Here's a simple way to give your monster a full mop on top. All you'll need is a crochet hook (about same size as your knitting needles) and a pair of scissors.

1. Cut a strand of contrasting-color yarn a few inches or centimeters in length. Insert the crochet hook under a bar that appears between two stitches on the main piece, and hook the folded piece of contrasting yarn onto it.

2. Draw the crochet hook out from under the bar on the main piece, pulling the contrasting yarn partway out.

3. Remove the crochet hook and insert the two tail ends through the loop. Pull to tighten the knot.

4. To make the knot less visible, poke it down into the main piece using a closed pair of scissors. Then trim the strands of yarn to the desired length.

MAGIC LOOP KNITTING

All the patterns in this book call for knitting with double-pointed needles, but if you prefer knitting with a circular needle, you can also knit the small circumferences of most toys using this method. Use a circular needle several inches or centimeters longer than the maximum circumference of the pieces you will knit (but don't worry about getting this measurement exactly right).

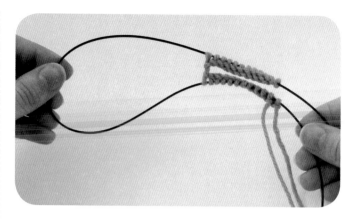

3. Pull on the cable between the stitches until you have pulled out a big loop.

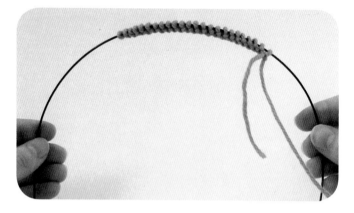

1. After casting on the designated number of stitches, slide all the stitches down onto the flexible plastic cable.

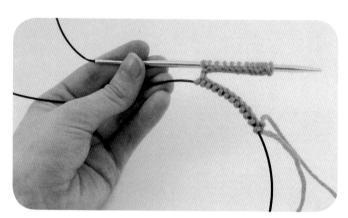

4. Slip the half of the stitches without the yarn connected (the top group of stitches) down to one end of the needle. Keep the half with the yarn connected (the bottom group of stitches) on the cable, while still keeping the loop pulled out between the two groups of stitches.

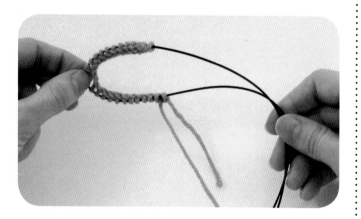

2. Divide the stitches into two groups, and fold the plastic in half between them, with the yarn attached to the group on the bottom. Grab onto the cable between the two groups of stitches.

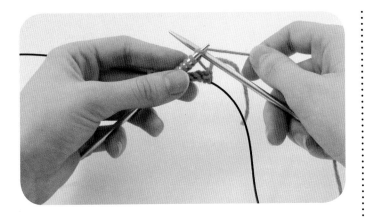

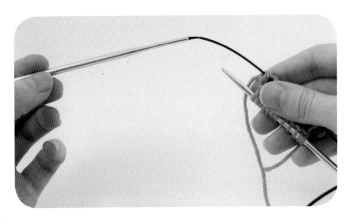

5. Align the cast-on sides of your stitches so that your knitting won't be twisted. Then, knit the stitches onto the empty end of the needle held in your right hand. You will have two loops of plastic cable on either side of your knitting.

7. Slide the stitches you just finished knitting (with the yarn attached) down onto the cable.

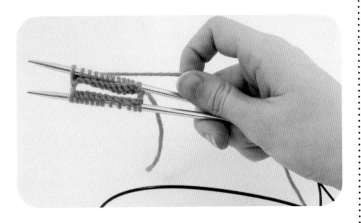

6. Once you finish knitting this half of the stitches, slide the other half of the stitches down to the other end of the needle, so that the two groups of stitches are on the two ends of the needle.

8. Flip the needle around so that the stitches are positioned as they were in Step 5, and knit the second set of stitches. Repeat Steps 5 to 8 to knit in the round. After a few rounds, you will see your circular piece take shape.

OLD-SCHOOL GHOULS

These guys never get old—mainly because they're already dead.

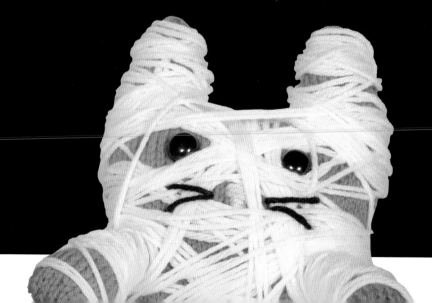

VAMPIRE BRATS

Big, looming vampires are terrifying, but the playground set are just little terrors! They're always crying for more bottles of blood, and you don't even want to hear about what happened to the family gerbil.

BABY VAMPIRE

BODY

With A, cast on 6 stitches onto 3 DPNs and join in a round.

RND 1: [Kfb] 6 times (12 sts).

RND 2: [Kfb, k1] 6 times (18 sts).

RND 3 AND ALL ODD-NUMBERED RNDS THROUGH RND 29: Knit.

RND 4: [Kfb, k2] 6 times (24 sts).

RND 6: [Kfb, k3] 6 times (30 sts).

RND 8: [Kfb, k4] 6 times (36 sts).

RND 10: [Kfb, k5] 6 times (42 sts).

Switch to B after Rnd 11.

RNDS 12–21: Knit (10 rnds).

RND 22: [K2tog, k5] 6 times (36 sts).

RND 24: [K2tog, k4] 6 times (30 sts).

RND 26: [K2tog, k3] 6 times (24 sts).

RND 28: [K2tog, k2] 6 times (18 sts).

Stuff the piece and attach eyes, placed about 10 stitches above the color change and spaced 6 stitches apart.

RND 30: [K2tog] 9 times (9 sts).

Break yarn and draw tightly through the stitches with a tapestry needle.

LEFT EAR (VAMPIRE'S LEFT)

Hold the body so that it's facing you, and with B, pick up and knit 5 stitches at the side of the head, about 3 stitches back from the eye. The knit side of these stitches should face forward (page 40).

Turn and purl.

NEXT ROW: [K2tog] twice, k1(3 sts).

Break yarn and draw tightly through the stitches with a tapestry needle, from right to left on the knit side.

RIGHT EAR (VAMPIRE'S RIGHT)

With B, pick up and knit 5 stitches at the side of the head, opposite the left ear.

Turn and purl.

NEXT ROW: K1, [k2tog] twice (3 sts).

Break yarn and draw tightly through the stitches with a tapestry needle, from right to left on the knit side (B page 40).

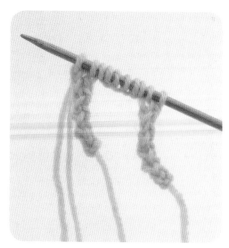

(C) You will join the two bib flaps into one piece by casting on stitches between them.

A For the left ear, pick up and knit stitches from the bottom of the ear to the top.

BABY'S ARMS/LEGS (MAKE 4)

With B, cast on 6 stitches onto 3 DPNs, leaving a tail for attaching, and join in a round.

FIRST RND: [Kfb, k1] 3 times (9 sts).

Knit 6 rounds.

Stuff piece, then break yarn and draw tightly through the stitches with a tapestry needle.

BIB

With C, cast on 2 stitches onto one needle, leaving a long tail.

Beginning with a purl row, work 9 rows in stockinette stitch.

Break yarn and set aside.

Make another piece the same as the first, without breaking the yarn.

Knit one more row, then cast on 6 stitches using the backward loop method.

Pick up the 2 stitches you set aside, and knit them, joining them with the stitches you just cast on. You now have 10 stitches on your needle (**C**).

ROWS 1–5: Turn and, beginning with a purl row, work 5 rows in stockinette stitch.

ROW 6: K1, k2tog, k4, k2tog, k1 (8 sts).

ROW 7: Purl.

ROW 8: K1, k2tog, k2, k2tog, k1(6 sts).

Bind off all stitches on the purl side.

B For the right ear, pick up and knit stitches from the top of the ear to the bottom.

BOTTLE

With D, cast on 6 stitches onto 3 DPNs and join in a round.

FIRST RND: [Kfb, k1] 3 times (9 sts).

Knit 7 rounds.

Bind off all stitches.

NIPPLE

With C, cast on 10 stitches onto 3 DPNs, leaving a tail for seaming, and join in a round.

RND 1: Knit.

RND 2: [K2tog] 5 times (5 sts).

Place stitches onto one needle to work as an I-cord.

RND 3: K2tog, k1, k2tog (3 sts).

RND 4: Knit.

Break yarn and draw tightly through the stitches.

Stuff the bottle, and stitch the cast-on edge of the nipple to the bound-off edge of the bottle.

FINISHING BABY VAMPIRE

With E embroider the mouth and with A embroider the tooth with one long stitch for each.

For hair, cut one strand of E. Insert a crochet hook under a stitch at the top of the head, fold the yarn in half, and pull through the stitch. Tuck the loose ends of the yarn through the loop that you've made, and pull tightly.

Attach the arms and legs to the body using mattress stitch.

Tie the bib around the body using the tail ends you left, then trim. With D, embroider two vertical stitches onto the bib to look like dripping blood. Make the stitches go through the body so that they also secure the bib to the body.

Attach the bottle to the hand with a couple of small stitches.

Weave in loose ends.

TODDLER VAMPIRE

BODY

With D, cast on 6 stitches onto 3 DPNs and join in a round.

RND 1: [Kfb] 6 times (12 sts).

RND 2: [Kfb, k1] 6 times (18 sts).

RND 3 AND ALL ODD-NUMBERED RNDS THROUGH RND 11: Knit.

RND 4: [Kfb, k2] 6 times (24 sts).

RND 6: [Kfb, k3] 6 times (30 sts).

RND 8: [Kfb, k4] 6 times (36 sts).

RND 10: [Kfb, k5] 6 times (42 sts).

RNDS 12–20: Knit (9 rnds).

Switch to B.

RNDS 21–28: Knit (8 rnds).

RND 29: [K2tog, k5] 6 times (36 sts).

RND 30 AND ALL EVEN-NUMBERED RNDS THROUGH RND 36: Knit.

RND 31: [K2tog, k4] 6 times (30 sts).

RND 33: [K2tog, k3] 6 times (24 sts).

RND 35: [K2tog, k2] 6 times (18 sts).

Stuff the piece and attach the eyes, placed about 10 stitches above the color change and spaced 6 stitches apart.

RND 37: [K2tog] 9 times (9 sts).

Break yarn and draw tightly through the stitches with a tapestry needle.

TODDLER'S ARMS/LEGS (MAKE 4)

With B, cast on 6 stitches onto 3 DPNs, leaving a tail for attaching, and join in a round.

FIRST RND: [Kfb, k1] 3 times (9 sts).

Knit 9 rounds.

Stuff the piece, then break yarn and draw tightly through the stitches with a tapestry needle.

FINISHING TODDLER VAMPIRE

Work Toddler Vampire's ears the same way as the Baby Vampire's.

With E and A, embroider the mouth and 2 teeth with one long stitch for each.

With E, embroider the hair with 3 long diagonal stitches.

With A, embroider a row of buttons with 2 stitches for each.

Attach the arms and legs to the body using mattress stitch.

For overall straps, with D, pick up and knit 2 stitches at the top of one side of the D section on the body, close to the arm ( page 42).

Knit 12 rows of I-cord, or make an I-cord that is long enough to reach over the

arm and down to top of D section on the back.

Bind off 2 stitches, then use the tail end to attach to the back (**E**). Repeat on the other side for the second strap.

TORN TEDDY BEAR

With F, cast on 6 stitches onto 3 DPNs and join in a round.

RND 1: [Kfb] 6 times (12 sts).
RND 2: [Kfb, k1] 6 times (18 sts).
RNDS 3–9: Knit (7 rnds).
RND 10: [K2tog] 3 times, BO 7, [k2tog] twice (6 sts).
RND 11: [Kfb] 3 times, cast on 6 sts, [kfb] 3 times (18 sts).
RNDS 12–15: Knit.
RND 16: [K2tog, k1] 6 times (12 sts).
RND 17: [K2tog] 6 times (6 sts).

Break yarn and draw tightly through the stitches with a tapestry needle.

Attach eyes 3 stitches down from the top of the head and spaced 3 stitches apart.

Stuff the piece through the side of the neck.

TEDDY'S EARS (MAKE 2)

Turn the body horizontally so that it faces you, and with F pick up and knit 4 stitches at the side of the head.

Turn and purl.
NEXT ROW: [K2tog] twice (2 sts).

Break yarn and draw tightly through the stitches with a tapestry needle.

TEDDY'S ARMS/LEGS (MAKE 4)

With F, pick up and knit 3 stitches at the side or the bottom of the body.

Knit 4 rows of I-cord, then break yarn and draw tightly through the stitches.

FINISHING TORN TEDDY BEAR

With E, embroider the nose with 2 horizontal stitches.

Weave in loose ends, and attach to the toddler's arm with a few stitches.

D To make the Toddler's overall straps, pick up and knit 2 stitches from the body to work as an I-cord.

E After making the I-cord for the overall straps, sew the bound-off end to the other side of the body.

SARCOPHACAT

What lurks underneath those mysterious wrappings?
Is it an undead kitty come to life via a curse on an ancient bag of catnip, or is it just a curious cat who's spent too much time in the yarn basket?

TECHNIQUES
Separating pieces (page 29), Kitchener stitch (page 140), mattress stitch (page 23)

YARN
Worsted-weight yarn in a main color, white and small amounts of pink and black

Samples knit with Cascade 220, 100% wool, 3½ oz (100g), 220 yds (201m), 1 skein or less 8891 Cyan Blue (MC), 8505 White (A), small amount 9477 Tutu (B), 8555 Black (C)

NEEDLES
Set of size 5 US (3.75mm) double-pointed needles

OTHER MATERIALS AND TOOLS
Size 15mm safety eyes, stuffing

FINISHED SIZE
Approx 7½" (19cm) tall

GAUGE
2" (5cm) = 11 stitches and 15½ rows in stockinette stitch (knit on RS, purl on WS)

NOTE: When wrapped with yarn, Sarcophacat is more appropriate for display; just leave the wrappings off for a rough-and-tumble feline friend.

BODY

With MC, cast on 6 stitches onto 3 DPNs and join to work in a round.

RND 1: [Kfb] 6 times (12 sts).

RND 2: [Kfb, k1] 6 times (18 sts).

RND 3 AND ALL ODD-NUMBERED RNDS THROUGH RND 27: Knit.

RND 4: [Kfb, k2] 6 times (24 sts).

RND 6: [Kfb, k3] 6 times (30 sts).

RND 8: [Kfb, k4] 6 times (36 sts).

RND 10: [Kfb, k5] 6 times (42 sts).

RND 12: [Kfb, k6] 6 times (48 sts).

RND 14: Knit.

RND 16: [Kfb, k7] 6 times (54 sts).

RND 18: Knit.

RND 20: [Kfb, k8] 6 times (60 sts).

RND 22: Knit.

RND 24: [Kfb, k9] 6 times (66 sts).

RND 26: Knit.

RND 28: [Kfb, k10] 6 times (72 sts).

RNDS 29–58: Knit (30 rnds).

RND 59: K14, BO 8 (begin binding off with 15th and 16th sts), k27, BO 8, k13.

You will now have a group of 28 stitches at the middle of the round separated from the other stitches by two sections of bound-off stitches. Place these stitches on a spare needle to work later.

Distribute the first 14 and the last 14 stitches of the round onto 3 DPNs—you will continue to work them in a round, joining them together at the gap that separates them, to form the left ear.

LEFT EAR

RND 60: K2tog, k10, [k2tog] twice, k10, k2tog (24 sts).

RNDS 61 AND 62: Knit.

RND 63: K2tog, k8, [k2tog] twice, k8, k2tog (20 sts).

RNDS 64 AND 65: Knit.

RND 66: K2tog, k6, [k2tog] twice, k6, k2tog (16 sts).

RNDS 67 AND 68: Knit.

RND 69: K2tog, k4, [k2tog] twice, k4, k2tog (12 sts).

RNDS 70 AND 71: Knit.

RND 72: [K2tog] 6 times (6 sts).

Break yarn and draw tightly through the stitches with a tapestry needle.

RIGHT EAR

Rejoin yarn with the last of the held stitches (the rightmost stitch on the purl side).

Distribute stitches onto 3 DPNs, and continue to work these stitches in a round, beginning by closing the gap that separates the last and the first stitch.

RND 73: K2tog, k10, [k2tog] twice, k10, k2tog (24 sts).

RNDS 74 AND 75: Knit.

RND 76: K2tog, k8, [k2tog] twice, k8, k2tog (20 sts).

RNDS 77 AND 78: Knit.

RND 79: K2tog, k6, [k2tog] twice, k6, k2tog (16 sts).

RNDS 80 AND 81: Knit.

RND 82: K2tog, k4, [k2tog] twice, k4, k2tog (12 sts).

RNDS 83 AND 84: Knit.

RND 85: [K2tog] 6 times (6 sts).

Break yarn and draw tightly through the stitches with a tapestry needle.

ARMS (MAKE 2)

With MC, cast on 12 stitches onto 3 DPNs, leaving a tail for seaming, and join to work in a round.

RNDS 1–12: Knit.

RND 13: [Kfb] twice, k2, [kfb] 4 times, k2, [kfb] twice (20 sts).

RNDS 14–19: Knit (6 rnds).

RND 20: [K2tog] twice, k2, [k2tog] 4 times, k2, [k2tog] twice (12 sts).

RND 21: Knit.

Divide stitches onto 2 DPNs and bind off using Kitchener stitch.

TAIL

With MC, cast on 14 stitches onto 3 needles, leaving a tail for seaming, and join to work in a round.

RNDS 1–38: Knit.

RND 39: [K2tog] 7 times (7 sts).

Break yarn and draw tightly through the stitches with a tapestry needle.

FINISHING

Attach eyes to the body, placed 10 stitches down from bound-off stitches and spaced 9 stitches apart. Stuff the body fully, making sure to fill out the ears, and seam the bound-off stitches using mattress stitch.

Stuff the arms, and with the tails left for seaming, attach the cast-on edges to the body, 10 stitches below the eyes and spaced a little wider than the eyes.

Stuff the tail, and with the yarn tail that you left for seaming, attach the cast-on edge to the back of the body, at the place where the increase rounds begin to be spaced 4 rounds apart.

With B, embroider the nose with 5 horizontal stitches (3 longer on top and 2 shorter on bottom), placed between and 3 rounds below the eyes.

Weave in loose ends.

With A, wrap the body in a random way, however you like, avoiding covering the eyes and nose. (I started with the tail and worked my way up, but the more random the wrap, the more mummylike your Sarcophacat will look.)

After you finish wrapping your cat, weave in the loose end of White in the wrappings.

With C, embroider 2 whiskers on each side of the nose, stitching through the body and on top of the wrapping.

EEK!
A naked sarcophacat
is best for play . . .

BITTY WITCHES

These green gals finally mastered the spell for shrinking!

Unfortunately, they forgot the spell for growing, and now they're eternally on dusting duty. Hang them perched on their broom for a cute Halloween decoration.

· · · · · F A C T S · · · · · ·

LIKES: The annual broom rodeo
HATES: Dust busters
EATS: Eye of shrimp
HAUNTS: The utility closet

WITCH

BODY

With B, cast on 4 stitches onto one needle.

RND 1 (WORK AS AN I-CORD): [Kfb] 4 times (8 sts).

Distribute stitches onto 3 DPNs and continue to work in a round.

RND 2: [Kfb] 8 times (16 sts).

RND 3: Knit.

RND 4: [Kfb, k1] 8 times (24 sts).

RND 5: Knit.

RND 6: [K2tog, yo] 12 times (24 sts).

RNDS 7–9: Knit.

RND 10: [K2tog, k2] 6 times (18 sts).

RNDS 11–14: Knit.

Switch to A.

RNDS 15–19: Knit (5 rnds).

RND 20: [K2tog, k1] 6 times (12 sts).

Stuff piece.

RND 21: [K2tog] 6 times.

Break yarn and draw tightly through the stitches with a tapestry needle.

EYES

With B, embroider eyes with 2 stitches for each, placed 3 stitches above the last color change and spaced 3 stitches apart.

ARMS

With A, cast on 2 stitches onto one needle.

Knit 18 rows of I-cord, then break yarn and draw tightly through the stitches with a tapestry needle.

With the end still threaded on the tapestry needle, insert the I-cord through the body, going in and coming out just under the color change and just outside the eyes. Pull the I-cord halfway through, so that an equal length sticks out from each side.

Weave loose ends back through the I-cord and the body.

FEET

With A, cast on 2 stitches onto one needle.

Knit 10 rows of I-cord, then break yarn and draw tightly through the stitches with a tapestry needle.

TECHNIQUES

I-cord (page 138), I-cord appendages (page 22), attaching hair (page 33), reverse Kitchener stitch (page 50)

YARN FOR WITCH

Fingering-weight yarn in green and black

SUPER FINE

Samples knit with Cascade Heritage, 75% wool, 25% nylon, 3½ oz (100g), 437 yds (400m), 1 skein or less each 5659 Primavera (A), 5601 Black (B)

YARN FOR BROOM

Worsted-weight yarn in brown and yellow

MEDIUM

Samples knit with Cascade 220, 100% wool, 3½ oz (100g), 220 yds (201m), 1 skein or less each 9471 Amber (C), 7827 Goldenrod (D)

NEEDLES FOR WITCH

Set of size 1 US (2.25mm) double-pointed needles

NEEDLES FOR BROOM

Set of size 5 US (3.75mm) double-pointed needles

OTHER MATERIALS AND TOOLS

Stuffing, small crochet hook (for attaching hair)

FINISHED SIZE

Witch is approx 1¾" (4.5cm) tall (not including hat); Broom is approx 5" (12.5cm) long

GAUGE FOR WITCH

2" (5cm) = 19 stitches and 23 rows in stockinette stitch (knit on RS, purl on WS)

GAUGE FOR BROOM

2" (5cm) = 11 stitches and 15½ rows in stockinette stitch (knit on RS, purl on WS)

NOTE: The Witches are very small and are not suitable for kids aged three and under.

With the end still threaded on the tapestry needle, insert the I-cord into one yarn-over hole in the skirt directly below one eye, and pull the end out through another yarn-over hole under the other eye. (There should be one yarn-over hole in between.) Pull the I-cord halfway through, so that an equal amount sticks out from each side. Weave loose ends back through the I-cord and the body.

NOSE
With A, cast on 2 stitches onto one needle.

Knit 2 rows of I-cord, then break yarn and draw tightly through the stitches with a tapestry needle.

With the end still threaded on the tapestry needle, insert the tip of the I-cord between and just under the eyes.

Without pulling the piece into the face, secure by weaving the end through the body a few times. Weave the loose end from the cast-on through the nose and the body.

HAIR
Cut 5 strands of B about 2" (5cm) long. Insert a crochet hook under a stitch at the top of the head, and use it to pull through a strand of yarn that you've folded in half. Tuck the loose ends of the yarn through the loop that you've pulled through, and pull tightly. Repeat with the other 4 strands.

Use the tip of a pair of sharp scissors to separate the individual strands of hair for a shaggy look. Trim to desired length.

HAT
With B, cast on 32 stitches onto 3 DPNs and join to work in a round.

RND 1: Knit.
RND 2: [K2tog, k2] 8 times (24 sts).
RND 3: Knit.
RND 4: [K2tog, k1] 8 times (16 sts).
RNDS 5–10: Knit.
RND 11: [K2tog, k2] 4 times (12 sts).
RNDS 12 AND 13: Knit.
RND 14: [K2tog] 6 times (6 sts).

Break yarn and draw tightly through the stitches with a tapestry needle.

Bend the top of the hat down and stitch in place with the loose end. Stitch to the top of the Witch's head.

FINISHING
Weave in loose ends.

BROOM
With C, cast on 6 stitches onto 3 DPNs and join in a round.

RND 1: [Kfb, k1] 3 times (9 sts).
RNDS 2–27: Knit.

Stuff the piece so far, and switch to D (without breaking C).

RND 28: Knit.
RND 29: [Kfb] to end (18 sts).
RND 30: [K1, p1] to end.

RND 31: Kfb, [p1, k1] 3 times, p1, [kfb] twice, [k1, p1] 3 times, k1, kfb (22 sts).
RND 32: [P1, k1] to end.

Switch to C (without breaking D).

RND 33: Knit.

Switch to D (and break C).

RND 34: Knit.
RND 35: Kfb, [k1, p1] 4 times, k1, [kfb] twice, [p1, k1] 4 times, p1, kfb (26 sts).
RND 36: [K1, p1] to end.
RNDS 37–41: Work 5 rounds in established rib pattern.
RNDS 42 AND 43: Purl.

Divide stitches onto 2 needles, and bind off with reverse Kitchener stitch (see above). Stuff the piece before closing up.

FINISHING
Weave in loose ends.

Stitch Witch to the broom at the arms, legs, or skirt, if desired.

Seaming the Broom with reverse Kitchener stitch gives a seamless, purled effect.

Every day is a
BAD HAIR DAY
for Bitty witches. Yikes!

WHAT-TO-WEREWOLF

···········

This teenage werewolf didn't feel like waiting for the full moon every month, so he figured out a way to frighten with fashion. Just a flip of the hood and some furry gloves are all it takes to transform him into the terror of his homeroom . . . or maybe just the class clown.

···········•···········

FACTS

LIKES: Reading *Howl*
HATES: The conformist cool kids, a.k.a. the "sheep"
EATS: Wolfgang Puck frozen pizzas
HAUNTS: The shopping maul

BODY

WORK LEGS

With A, cast on 8 stitches onto 3 DPNs and join to work in a round.

FIRST RND: [Kfb] 8 times (16 sts).

Knit 16 rounds.

Break yarn, and set these 16 stitches aside on a holder or a pair of spare needles.

Make another leg the same as above, without breaking the yarn.

Distribute the stitches of both legs onto 2 needles, with the first 8 stitches of each leg on one needle and the second 8 stitches of each leg on another. Hold the needles so that the working yarn is attached to the rightmost stitch on the back needle.

Knit one round, starting with the needle in front, then flipping needles around and continuing on with the back needle.

Distribute 32 stitches onto 3 DPNs to continue to work in a round.

SHAPE TORSO

RNDS 1–3: Knit.

Stuff the piece so far, and switch to B (and break A).

RNDS 4 AND 5: Knit.

RNDS 6 AND 7: Switch to C, and knit.

RNDS 8 AND 9: Switch to B, and knit.

RNDS 10 AND 11: Switch to C, and knit.

RNDS 12 AND 13: Switch to B, and knit.

RNDS 14 AND 15: Switch to C, and knit.

Switch to B (and break C).

RND 16: Knit.

RND 17: [K2tog] twice, k8, [k2tog] 4 times, k8, [k2tog] twice (24 sts).

Switch to D (and break B).

RND 18: [K2tog, k1] to end (16 sts).

RND 19: [Kfb] 16 times (32 sts).

RND 20: Knit.

RND 21: [Kfb, k3] 8 times (40 sts).

RNDS 22–29: Knit (8 rnds).

RND 30: [K2tog, k3] 8 times (32 sts).

TECHNIQUES

Joining pieces (page 28), I-cord (page 138), picking up stitches (page 30), Kitchener stitch (page 140), mattress stitch (page 23), backstitch (page 26), slip slip knit (page 136)

YARN

Worsted-weight yarn in 6 colors plus a small amount of black

Samples knit with Cascade 220, 100% wool, 3½ oz (100g), 220 yds (201m) 1 skein or less each 7815 Summer Sky (A), 7814 Chartreuse (B), 8505 White (C), 8021 Beige (D), 9471 Amber (E), 7825 Orange Sherbet (F), 8555 Black (G)

NEEDLES

Set of size 5 US (3.75mm) double-pointed needles

OTHER MATERIALS AND TOOLS

Size 9mm safety eyes, stuffing

FINISHED SIZE

Approx 7½" (19cm) tall

GAUGE

2" (5cm) = 11 stitches and 15½ rows in stockinette stitch (knit on RS, purl on WS)

RNDS 31 AND 32: Knit.

RND 33: [K2tog, k2] 8 times (24 sts).

RNDS 34 AND 35: Knit.

Finish stuffing the piece, leaving the body on the slimmer side to ensure that the jacket will be a good fit.

RND 36: [K2tog, k1] 8 times (16 sts).

Attach the eyes, placed 5 stitches above the last increase round and spaced 5 stitches apart.

RND 37: [K2tog] 8 times (8 sts).

Break yarn and draw tightly through the stitches with a tapestry needle.

FEET (MAKE 2)

With C, cast on 6 stitches onto 3 DPNs, leaving a tail for seaming, and join to work in a round.

Who needs a leather
jacket when you can go
LUPINE?

RND 1: [Kfb] 6 times (12 sts).

RND 2: Knit.

RND 3: K3, kfb, k1, [kfb] twice, k1, kfb, k3 (16 sts).

RNDS 4–9: Knit (6 rnds).

RND 10: K3, k2tog, k1, [k2tog] twice, k1, k2tog, k3 (12 sts).

RND 11: Knit.

Stuff the piece.

RND 12: [K2tog] 6 times (6 sts).

Break yarn and draw tightly through the stitches with a tapestry needle.

ARMS (MAKE 2)

With B, cast on 6 stitches onto 3 needles, leaving a tail for seaming, and join to work in a round.

RND 1: [Kfb] to end (12 sts).

Switch to C (without breaking B).

RNDS 2 AND 3: Knit.

Switch to B (and break C).

RNDS 4 AND 5: Knit.

Switch to D (and break B).

RNDS 6–23: Knit (18 rnds).

Stuff the piece.

RND 24: [K2tog] to end (6 sts).

Break yarn and draw tightly through the stitches with a tapestry needle.

HAIR

With E, cast on 14 stitches onto one needle using the backward loop method to work straight.

ROWS 1–4: Beginning with a knit row, work 4 rows in stockinette stitch.

ROW 5: K1, k2tog, k to last 3 sts, k2tog, k1 (12 sts).

ROWS 6–8: Continue in stockinette stitch for 3 rows.

ROW 9: Work same as Row 5 (10 sts).

ROWS 10–12: Continue in stockinette stitch for 3 rows.

ROW 13: K1, k2tog, k to end (9 sts).

ROW 14: Purl.

ROW 15: K1, k2tog, k to end (8 sts).

ROWS 16–20: Continue in stockinette stitch for 5 rows.

ALTERNATIVE KITCHENER STITCH

When seaming together the tops of the stitches on the jacket (to form a tank top–like piece), you will use a slightly altered Kitchener stitch. Because the tail end is attached to the front right stitch instead of the back right stitch (as it usually is in Kitchener stitch), the order of stitching will be one off: first slip the needle knitwise through the back right stitch, then purlwise through the front right stitch. Next, insert the needle purlwise through the back right stitch and slip off, then knitwise through the following back right stitch. Continue as established.

ROW 21: K1, k2tog, k2, k2tog, k1 (6 sts)

Bind off all stitches purlwise.

FINISHING BODY

Weave in loose ends, except for the tails you left for seaming.

Attach arms to the top of the B/C section on the body at a downward angle using mattress stitch.

Attach feet to the bottoms of the legs using mattress stitch, with the closed-up end of the feet facing forward.

Place hair on top of the head, with the cast-on edge angled across the forehead and back to one side. Attach to the head using backstitch.

Weave in remaining loose ends.

JACKET

With F, cast on 36 stitches onto 3 DPNs and join to work in a round.

RNDS 1–14: K8, p2, k to end.

WORK FRONT LEFT SIDE

LF ROW 15: K1, [k2tog] twice, k1, ssk, k1 (6 sts). Turn to work these 6 stitches separately, leaving the remaining stitches on the needles to work later.

LF ROW 16: Purl.

LF ROW 17: K1, k2tog, ssk, k1 (4 sts).

LF ROW 18: Purl.

LF ROW 19: K1, ssk, k1 (3 sts)

LF ROWS 20–24: Continue in stockinette stitch for 5 rows, ending with a purl row.

Break yarn, leaving a tail for seaming, and place stitches on a scrap piece of yarn to work later.

WORK FRONT RIGHT SIDE

Reattach yarn to the next live stitch, which was previously the second purl when you were working in the round.

RF ROW 15: K1, k2tog, k1, [ssk] twice, k1 (6 sts). Turn to work these 6 stitches separately, leaving the remaining stitches on one needle to work later.

RF ROW 16: Purl.

RF ROW 17: K1, k2tog, ssk, k1 (4 sts).

RF ROW 18: Purl.

RF ROW 19: K1, k2tog, k1 (3 sts).

RF ROWS 20–24: Continue in stockinette stitch for 5 rows, ending with a purl row.

Break yarn, leaving a tail for seaming, and place stitches on a scrap piece of yarn to work later.

WORK BACK SIDE

Reattach yarn to the next live stitch.

BACK ROW 15: K1, [k2tog] twice, k8, [ssk] twice, k1 (14 sts).

BACK ROW 16: Purl.

BACK ROW 17: K1, k2tog, k8, ssk, k1 (12 sts).

BACK ROWS 18–23: Continue in stockinette stitch for 6 rows.

BACK ROW 24: P3, BO 6 (begin binding off with 4th and 5th sts), p2.

NOTE: There should now be 2 sets of 3 stitches on either end of the working needle.

A Thread the tail end from the front left-side stitches onto a tapestry needle, and seam these stitches with the corresponding back stitches using alternative Kitchener stitch (page 55).

B To begin knitting the sleeves, pick up and knit 16 stitches around the armhole. It's easiest to pick up stitches using 2 DPNs, then distribute them onto 3 DPNs to work in a round.

Place the stitches that are being held on scrap yarn onto one needle, and hold that needle parallel to the one with the back stitches (**A**).

Use alternative Kitchener stitch (page 55) to seam together the front and back of each shoulder.

Once you have finished seaming, the piece will look like a sleeveless shirt.

SLEEVES (MAKE 2)

With F, pick up and knit 16 stitches around the armhole, beginning at the bottom middle of the hole (**B**).

Knit 16 rounds, then bind off all stitches.

HOOD

With E, cast on 38 stitches onto one needle to work straight.

ROW 1: K1, [yo, k2tog] 9 times, [k2tog, yo] 9 times, k1.

ROWS 2–8: Beginning with a purl row, work 7 rows in stockinette stitch.

ROW 9: K17, [k2tog] twice, k17 (36 sts).

ROW 10: Purl.

ROW 11: K16, [k2tog] twice, k16 (34 sts).

ROW 12: Purl.

ROW 13: K15, [k2tog] twice, k15 (32 sts).

ROW 14: Purl.

ROW 15: K12, [k2tog] 4 times, k12 (28 sts).

ROW 16: Purl.

ROW 17: K10, [k2tog] 4 times, k10 (24 sts).

ROW 18: Purl.

ROW 19: K8, [k2tog] 4 times, k8 (20 sts).

Divide stitches onto 2 DPNs, and bind off using regular Kitchener stitch.

SNOUT

With E, pick up and knit 6 stitches at the middle of the cast-on edge of the hood (**C**).

ROW 1: Turn and purl.

ROW 2: K1, [k2tog] twice, k1 (4 sts).

ROW 3: Purl.

ROW 4: Knit.

Switch to G.

ROW 5: Knit (on purl side).

C To begin making the snout, pick up and knit 6 stitches on the cast-on edge of the hood.

ROW 6: [P2tog] twice.

Break yarn and draw tightly through the stitches with a tapestry needle.

EARS (MAKE 2)

Flip the hood so that the purl side faces out and the snout faces away from you. With E, pick up and knit 4 stitches, placed 8 rows back from the cast-on edge of the hood and 4 stitches outside the snout (**D**).

ROWS 1–3: Beginning with a purl row, work 3 rows in stockinette stitch.

ROW 4: [K2tog] twice (2 sts).

ROW 5: Purl.

Break yarn and draw tightly through the stitches with a tapestry needle.

GLOVES (MAKE 2)

With E, cast on 16 stitches onto 3 DPNs and join to work in a round.

RNDS 1 AND 2: [K1, p1] to end.

RNDS 3–5: Knit.

RND 6: [Kfb, k7] twice (18 sts).

RNDS 7–10: Knit.

RND 11: [K2tog] 9 times (9 sts).

Break yarn and draw tightly through the stitches with a tapestry needle.

CLAWS (MAKE 2 PER GLOVE)

With C, cast on 2 stitches onto one needle.

Knit 8 rows of I-cord, then break yarn and draw tightly through the stitches with a tapestry needle.

With the end still threaded on the tapestry needle, insert the I-cord vertically under 2 bars between stitches just to one side of the closed-up stitches on the glove. Pull the I-cord halfway through so that an equal length sticks out from each side, and weave in loose ends. Repeat with another I-cord for a total of 4 claws on each glove.

FINISHING JACKET

With the purl side of the hood and the knit side of the jacket facing out, attach the hood to the jacket using mattress stitch, beginning at a corner of the hood adjacent to the cast-on edge and one stitch outside of the front purl stitches on the jacket.

Cut a 10" (25.5cm) strand of E, thread it on a tapestry needle, and weave it in and out of the yarn-over holes next to the cast-on edge of the hood. Once you have threaded it all the way through, tie a knot in each end. When you gently tug on both ends of this yarn, the hood will tighten close to Wolfie's head.

Cut two shorter strands of E, and use a tapestry needle to thread one through the bottom of each glove and the bottom edge of the sleeve. Tie in a knot.

Weave in loose ends.

D To begin making an ear, pick up and knit 4 stitches on the top of the hood, with the snout facing away from you.

ZOMBIE SLEEPOVER

It's an undead pajama party! These rowdy zombies are up all night watching B movies, munching on deep-fried gray matter, and gossiping about who's lost which body part. But come morning, there will be lots of moaning and rolling over in their graves. Put the zombies to bed all snug in their close-able graves. This interactive knit can be a fun toy or a kooky centerpiece.

TECHNIQUES

Joining pieces (page 28), I-cord (page 138), I-cord appendages (page 22), backward loop cast-on (page 136), picking up stitches (page 30), Kitchener stitch (page 140), mattress stitch (page 23)

YARN FOR ZOMBIE

Fingering-weight yarn in pale green, camel, and black

Samples knit with Cascade Heritage, 75% wool, 25% nylon, 3½ oz (100g), 437 yds (400m), 1 skein or less each 5629 Citron (A), 5610 Camel (B), 5601 Black (C)

YARN FOR GRAVEYARD

Worsted-weight yarn in green, brown, gray, and black

Samples knit with Cascade 220, 100% wool, 3½ oz (100g), 220 yds (201m), 1 skein or less each 8894 Christmas Green (D), 8686 Brown (E), 8509 Grey (F), 8555 Black (G)

NEEDLES FOR ZOMBIE

Set of size 1 US (2.25mm) double-pointed needles

NEEDLES FOR GRAVEYARD

Set of size 5 US (3.75mm) double-pointed needles; 24" (61cm) size 5 US (3.75mm) circular needle (optional)

OTHER MATERIALS AND TOOLS

Crochet hook (for grass), stuffing

FINISHED SIZE

Zombie is approx 1" (2.5cm) tall; Graveyard is approx 9" (23 cm) long

GAUGE FOR ZOMBIE

2" (5cm) = 19 stitches and 23 rows in stockinette stitch (knit on RS, purl on WS)

GAUGE FOR GRAVEYARD

2" (5cm) = 11 stitches and 15½ rows in stockinette stitch (knit on RS, purl on WS)

NOTES: The Zombies are very small and are not suitable for kids aged three and under.

The optional circular needle is for knitting the ground using the magic loop technique (page 34), which makes the switch from circular to straight knitting easier.

FACTS

LIKES: Long lurches on the beach
HATES: Deep massages
EATS: Brains—or brain-flavored tofu when dieting
HAUNTS: Mensa meetings

Zombie
BODY

With A, cast on 4 stitches onto one needle.

Knit 3 rows of I-cord, then break yarn and set it aside on a spare needle.

Make a second leg the same way as the first, without breaking the yarn.

JOIN LEGS

Distribute the stitches of both legs onto two needles, with the first 2 stitches of each leg on one needle and the second 2 stitches of each leg on another. Hold the needles so that the working yarn is attached to the rightmost stitch on the back needle.

Switch to B (without breaking A). Knit one round, starting with the needle in front, then flipping needles around and continuing on with the back needle.

Distribute 8 stitches onto 3 DPNs to continue to work in a round.

SHAPE BODY

RND 1: [Kfb] 8 times (16 sts).
RND 2: Knit.
Switch to A (without breaking B).
RND 3: Knit.
RND 4: [K1 A, k1 B] to end.
Switch to B (without breaking A).
RNDS 5–7: Knit.
Switch to A (and break B).
RNDS 8–12: Knit (5 rnds).
Stuff piece.
RND 13: [K2tog] 8 times (8 sts).
Break yarn and draw tightly through the stitches with a tapestry needle.

EYES

With C, embroider the eyes with 2 stitches for each, placed 3 stitches above the last color change and spaced 2 stitches apart.

ARMS

With A, cast on 2 stitches onto one needle.

Knit 15 rows of I-cord, then break yarn and draw tightly through the stitches with a tapestry needle.

With the end still threaded on the tapestry needle, insert the I-cord through the body, going in and coming out just under the last color change and just outside the eyes. Pull the I-cord halfway through, so that an equal length sticks out from each side.

Weave loose ends back through the I-cord and the body, using one stitch to bend the tips of the arms down into a zombielike pose.

FINISHING ZOMBIE

For hair, use B to make several long stitches radiating out from the top of the head.

Weave in loose ends.

Graveyard
GROUND

With D, cast on 68 stitches onto 3 DPNs or circular needle, if using the magic loop method. Place beginning-of-round marker, and join to work in a round.

RNDS 1–8: Knit.

FORM HOLE 1

NEXT RND: K6, BO 10, k to end (58 sts).

Beginning with the next row, you will work the piece straight, turning on either side of the bound-off stitches to create a hole.

K6, then turn.

Beginning with a purl row, work 6 rows in stockinette stitch. (For this section, temporarily consider the stitch immediately to the right of the bound-off stitches to be the first stitch in the row, while leaving the original marker in place.)

NEXT RND: K6, cast on 10 stitches using backward loop, then knit to end of round (68 sts)

Knit 6 rounds.

FORM HOLE 2

NEXT RND: K20, BO 10, k to end (58 sts).

As with Hole 1, beginning with the next row, you will work the piece back and forth on either side of the bound-off stitches to create a hole.

K6, then turn.

Beginning with a purl row, work 6 rows in stockinette stitch.

NEXT RND: K20, cast on 10 stitches using the backward loop method, then knit to the end of the round (68 sts).

Knit 6 rounds.

FORM REMAINING HOLES

Begin again with Hole 1, and continue on to make another Hole 2 to form two more holes.

Repeat Hole 1 once more, finishing by knitting 6 rounds. You will have 5 holes total in the piece.

Divide the stitches into 2 sections (on 2 needles if you're using DPNs, and on either end of the needle if you're using a circular needle). Make sure that the beginning of the round matches up with the original beginning, and it's not beginning at one side of a hole. Bind off using Kitchener stitch.

(A) Seam the two ends of the ground piece with mattress stitch.

Lay the piece flat, and seam the cast-on edge using mattress stitch (**A**).

GRAVE DIRT (MAKE 5)

With E, cast on 10 stitches onto one needle to work straight.

Beginning with a purl row, work 8 rows in stockinette stitch.

Instead of turning for the next purl row, rotate the piece 90 degrees clockwise, and pick up and knit 5 stitches along the side of the piece with a second DPN. With a third DPN, pick up and knit 10 stitches from the cast-on edge. With a fourth DPN, pick up and knit 5 stitches along remaining side (**B**).

Redistribute the stitches onto 3 DPNs, and join to work in a round.

RNDS 1–3: Knit.

RND 4: K10, BO to end, and BO the last stitch using the first stitch of the round. You will have one stitch on your right needle and 9 stitches on your left.

Continue to knit to the end of the row. Turn the piece; you will then work the piece straight to form the flap of the grave.

ROW 1: K1, [kfb] twice, k4, [kfb] twice, k1 (14 sts).

ROWS 2–8: Beginning with a purl row, work 7 rows in stockinette stitch.

ROW 9: K1, [k2tog] twice, k2, yo, k2, [k2tog] twice, k1 (11 sts).

Bind off all stitches on purl side.

B After knitting the flat piece of dirt, pick up and knit stitches around the sides of the piece to continue to work in the round.

KNOB FOR FLAP

NOTE: You will be able to insert this piece into the yarn-over hole in the dirt flap to "close" the open grave.

Turn the grave dirt piece so that the flap is at the bottom, and the purl side of the rest of the piece faces you.

Pick up and knit 2 stitches at the middle top of the piece (**C**).

Knit 2 rows of I-cord.

NEXT ROW (WORK AS AN I-CORD): [Kfbf] twice (6 sts) (see opposite).

Break yarn, and draw tightly through the stitches, from right to left.

GRAVESTONE (MAKE 5)

With F, cast on 16 stitches onto 3 DPNs, leaving a tail for attaching.

RNDS 1–10: Knit.

NOTE: You can vary the heights of the graves by knitting 9 or 11 total rounds here instead of 10.

RND 11: K2tog, k4, [k2tog] twice, k4, k2tog (12 sts).

RND 12: Knit.

RND 13: K2tog, k2, [k2tog] twice, k2, k2tog (8 sts).

Divide the stitches onto 2 needles, and bind off using Kitchener stitch.

C Pick up two stitches on the piece of grave dirt to make a knot that will allow you to close the grave.

KFBF

Kfbf = Knit through the front and back of the stitch without slipping it off the left needle, then knit once more through the front of the stitch before slipping it off. This will make an increase of 2 stitches.

For eyes, use G to embroider 2 stitches for each eye, placed halfway down one side, and spaced 2 stitches apart.

DEAD TREE

With E, cast on 3 stitches onto one needle, leaving a tail for seaming. Knit 2 rows of I-cord, then break yarn and set aside on a needle.

Make another I-cord in the same way, and set aside. Make a third I-cord with 3 rows of knitting instead of 2, and leave the yarn attached.

JOIN ROOTS

Hold the I-cord with the yarn attached in your right hand. In your left, hold another I-cord, and knit the left-hand stitches onto the right needle, connecting the two pieces together as you do so (**D**).

D To begin the tree, connect two I-cords together, then add a third.

Pick up the remaining needle with an I-cord, and join by knitting these stitches onto the right needle.

Distribute 9 stitches onto 3 DPNs, and join to work in a round.

Knit 9 rounds.

NEXT RND: [K2tog, k1] 3 times (6 sts).

Knit one more round, then break yarn and draw tightly through the stitches with a tapestry needle.

For branches, make three 2-stitch I-cords of varying lengths of 10, 12, and 14 rows. Thread each I-cord through the top of the Tree, so that an equal length sticks out from each side. Weave in the loose ends, and use these ends to stuff the piece.

FINISHING GRAVEYARD

Weave in loose ends, except for the tails you left for seaming.

Orient the ground so that the row of 3 holes is in the back and the 2 holes are in the front. Insert the grave dirt into a hole, so that the purl side is concave and the flap is on the right. Thread a strand of E onto a tapestry needle, and use whipstitch to stitch it into the hole. When you reach the flap, stitch along the area where the flap extends beyond the rest of the dirt.

Before you sew in the last piece of grave dirt, stuff the ground so that it is filled out and firm while still retaining a more or less flat surface.

Lightly stuff the gravestones, pinch them flat, and attach them to the ground using mattress stitch. Make 2 rows of stitches, for the front and back of the grave, running parallel to each other.

Attach the tree to the ground with the tails you left on the I-cords.

For grass, cut a few strands of D and attach them randomly to the ground using a crochet hook.

Weave in remaining loose ends.

BACKYARD BEASTIES

Enjoy some locally harvested creepy crawlies, and just remember that they're more scared of you than you are of them. Or is it the other way around? They can never remember.

COMPACT FLUORESCENT EELS

The latest mutation in eel technology, CFEs harvest clean energy directly from the sun. Carbon footprint? They don't even have feet! Their efficient power is all the better to zap you with, of course.

•

BODY

With MC, cast on 6 stitches onto 3 DPNs and join to work in a round.

RNDS 1–3: Knit.

RND 4: [Kfb, k1] 3 times (9 sts).

RNDS 5–16: Knit (12 rnds).

RND 17: [Kfb, k2] 3 times (12 sts).

RNDS 18–29: Work color pattern (12 rnds).

NOTE: In Rows 1, 5, 8, and 12 of the color pattern, after each stitch of CC, knit 1 stitch with MC, then wrap CC once around MC before knitting the next stitch.

RND 30: [Kfb, k3] 3 times (15 sts).

RNDS 31–42: Knit (12 rnds).

RND 43: [Kfb, k4] 3 times (18 sts).

RNDS 44–55: Work color pattern (12 rnds).

EEL COLOR PATTERN

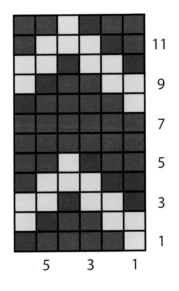

11

9

7

5

3

1

 5 3 1

Repeat these 6 stitches in the round

■ Knit with MC   □ Knit with CC

TECHNIQUES

Stranded colorwork (page 140), mattress stitch (page 23), picking up stitches (page 30)

YARN

Worsted-weight yarn in 2 colors

Samples knit with Cascade 220, 100% wool, 3½ oz (100g), 220 yds (201m), 1 skein or less 7803 Magenta (MC) or 7812 Lagoon (MC)

Bernat Glow in the Dark, 70% acrylic, 30% polyester, 1¾ oz (50g) and 90 yds (82m), 1 skein or less 54005 Glow White (CC)

NEEDLES

Set of 6" size 5 US (3.75mm) double-pointed needles

OTHER MATERIALS AND TOOLS

Size 9mm safety eyes, stuffing

FINISHED SIZE

Approx 13½" (34.5cm) long

GAUGE

2" (5cm) = 11 stitches and 15½ rows in stockinette stitch (knit on RS, purl on WS)

RND 56: [Kfb, k5] 3 times (21 sts).

RNDS 57–68: Knit (12 rnds).

RND 69: [Kfb, k6] 3 times (24 sts).

RNDS 70–81: Work color pattern (12 rnds).

RNDS 82 AND 83: Knit.

RND 84: [Kfb, k7] 3 times (27 sts).

RNDS 85 AND 86: Knit.

RND 87: [Kfb, k8] 3 times (30 sts).

RNDS 88 AND 89: Knit.

WORK TOP JAW

Knit 16, and place the 16 stitches onto one needle. Place the other 14 stitches on another needle to work later. You will now work the 16 stitches separately as a straight piece.

ROWS 90–93: Beginning with a knit row, work 4 rows in stockinette stitch.

ROW 94: K1, [k2tog, k2] 3 times, k2tog, k1 (12 sts).

ROWS 95–97: Continue in stockinette stitch for 3 rows.

ROW 98: K1, k2tog, k1, [k2tog] twice, k1, k2tog, k1 (8 sts).

ROW 99 AND ALL ODD-NUMBERED ROWS THROUGH ROW 107: Purl.

ROW 100: K1, k2tog, k2, k2tog, k1 (6 sts).

ROW 102: K1, [k2tog] twice, k1 (4 sts).

Switch to CC before Row 103.

ROW 104: K1, [kfb] twice, k1 (6 sts).

ROW 106: K1, kfb, k2, kfb, k1 (8 sts).

ROW 108: K1, kfb, k4, kfb, k1 (10 sts).

ROW 109–111: Continue in stockinette stitch for 3 rows.

ROW 112: K1, kfb, k6, kfb, k1 (12 sts).

ROWS 113–116: Continue in stockinette stitch for 4 rows, ending with a knit row.

Break yarn, and leave these 12 stitches on one needle to work later.

WORK BOTTOM JAW

Reattach MC to the rightmost stitch (on the knit side) of the 14 stitches on the other needle.

ROWS 117–120: Beginning with a knit row, work 4 rows in stockinette stitch.

ROW 121: K1, k2tog, k8, k2tog, k1 (12 sts).

ROW 122 AND ALL EVEN-NUMBERED ROWS THROUGH ROW 136: Purl.

ROW 123: K1, k2tog, k6, k2tog, k1 (10 sts).

ROW 125: K1, k2tog, k4, k2tog, k1 (8 sts).

ROW 127: K1, k2tog, k2, k2tog, k1 (6 sts).

ROW 129: K1, [k2tog] twice, k1 (4 sts).

Switch to CC before Row 130.

ROW 131: K1, [kfb] twice, k1 (6 sts).

ROW 133: K1, kfb, k2, kfb, k1 (8 sts).

ROW 135: K1, kfb, k4, kfb, k1 (10 sts).

ROW 137: K1, kfb, k6, kfb, k1 (12 sts).

ROWS 138–143: Continue in stockinette stitch for 6 rows, ending with a knit row.

JOIN JAWS

RND 144: Instead of turning for the next row, knit the 12 held stitches from the other needle, joining them with the stitches you had been working with. Then, flip the needles around, and continue to knit the 12 stitches of the bottom jaw, joining all 24 stitches into a round.

Distribute the stitches onto 3 DPNs and continue to work in a round.

RNDS 145 AND 146: Knit.

RND 147: [K2tog, k2] 6 times (18 sts).

RNDS 148–165: Knit (18 rnds).

RND 166: [K2tog, k1] 6 times (12 sts).

RNDS 167–172: Knit (6 rnds).

RND 173: [K2tog] 6 times (6 sts).

Break yarn and draw tightly through the stitches with a tapestry needle.

Attach the eyes to the MC section of the top jaw, 8 stitches back from the color change at the tip of the jaw, and spaced 4 stitches apart.

Lightly stuff the tail, and then insert the CC lining into the body, turning it inside out as you do so, so that the purl side of the lining faces the purl side of the main piece. Add more stuffing to the head, between the eyes, and between the two layers of the bottom jaw.

Attach the lining to the top and bottom jaws using mattress stitch, beginning at the top front of the jaw, sewing around to the bottom and continuing around the other side (**A**).

FINS (MAKE 2)

Turn the body so that the eyes face you, and with MC, pick up and knit 5 stitches at the side of the body, just in front of the last CC stripe. Pick up stitches so that the knit side faces forward (**B**).

Turn and, beginning with a purl row, work 3 rows in stockinette stitch.

NEXT ROW: K1, k3tog, k1 (3 sts).

Break yarn and draw tightly through the stitches with a tapestry needle.

FINISHING

Weave in loose ends.

Cut several strands of CC, and stitch them into the small cast-on opening at the tip of the tail.

Before you insert the lining into the body, the body and lining are attached at the lips as one piece.

A After inserting the lining inside the body, seam the lining to the mouth using mattress stitch.

B To begin making a fin, pick up and knit 5 stitches at the side of the body, just in front of the last stripe.

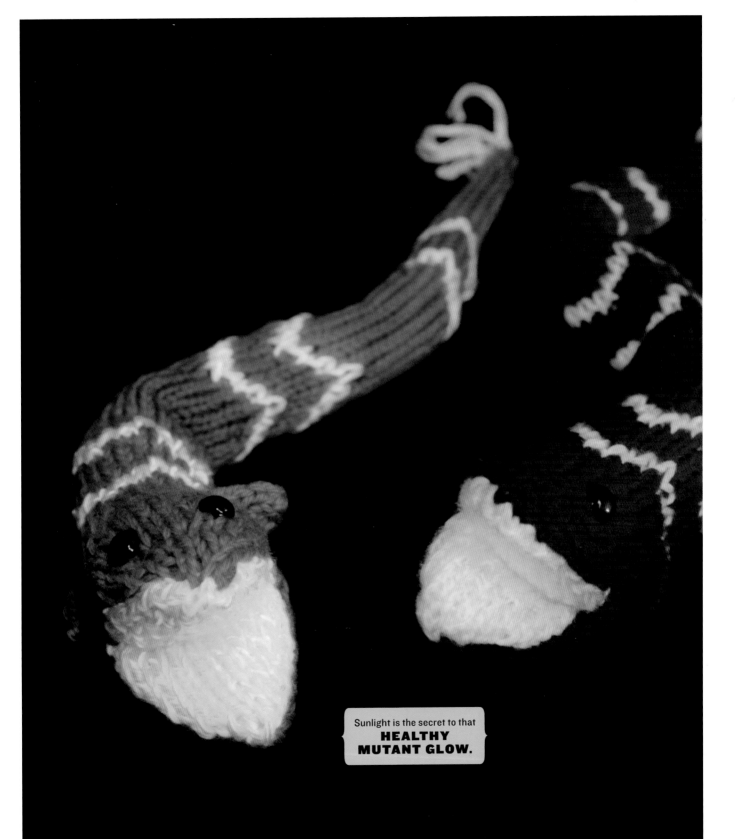

Sunlight is the secret to that
**HEALTHY
MUTANT GLOW.**

CONJOINED LAB RATS

Born joined at the tail, these tiny twin rats were placed in different groups in an obesity experiment before their big escape from the science lab. It turns out that nurture is just as important as nature, at least when it comes to rat waistlines.

TECHNIQUES

I-cord (page 138), picking up stitches (page 30), I-cord appendages (page 22)

YARN

Fingering-weight yarn in 2 colors

1 SUPER FINE

Samples knit with Cascade Heritage, 75% wool, 25% nylon, 3½ oz (100g), 437 yds (400m), 1 skein or less each 5618 Snow (MC), 5616 Fuchsia (CC)

NEEDLES

Set of size 1 US (2.25mm) double-pointed needles

OTHER MATERIALS AND TOOLS

Stuffing

FINISHED SIZE

Fat Rat is approx 1" (2.5cm) tall; Skinny Rat is approx 1½" (3.8cm) tall

GAUGE

2" (5cm) = 19 stitches and 23 rows in stockinette stitch (knit on RS, purl on WS)

NOTE: While appropriate for kitty, this project is very small and is not suitable for kids aged three and under.

· · · · · FACTS · · · · ·

LIKES: One likes exercise wheels, the other cheese wheels

HATES: Mazes

EATS: One eats green beans, the other jelly beans

HAUNTS: "Before & After" photo shoots

FAT RAT BODY

With MC, cast on 6 stitches onto 3 DPNs and join in a round.

RND 1: [Kfb] 6 times (12 sts).
RND 2: [Kfb, k1] 6 times (18 sts).
RND 3: Knit.
RND 4: [Kfb, k2] 6 times (24 sts).
RND 5: Knit.
RND 6: [Kfb, k3] 6 times (30 sts).
RNDS 7–12: Knit (6 rnds).
RND 13: [K2tog, k3] 6 times (24 sts).
RND 14: Knit.
RND 15: [K2tog, k2] 6 times (18 sts).
RND 16: Knit.
Stuff the piece.
RND 17: [K2tog, k1] 6 times (12 sts).
RND 18: [K2tog] 6 times.

Break yarn and draw tightly through the stitches with a tapestry needle.

SKINNY RAT BODY

With MC, cast on 6 stitches onto 3 DPNs and join in a round.

RND 1: [Kfb] 6 times (12 sts).
RND 2: [Kfb, k1] 6 times (18 sts).
RNDS 3–16: Knit (14 rnds).
Stuff the piece.
RND 17: [K2tog, k1] 6 times (12 sts).
RND 18: [K2tog] 6 times (6 sts).

Break yarn and draw tightly through the stitches with a tapestry needle.

FEATURES

With CC, embroider eyes with 2 small stitches for each. For the Fat Rat, eyes should be 6 stitches down from the top of the head and spaced 5 stitches apart. For the Skinny Rat, eyes should be 4 stitches from the top of the head and spaced 3 stitches apart.

Embroider the nose with 2 small stitches directly between and just below eyes.

EARS (MAKE 2 PER BODY)

With CC, pick up and knit 4 stitches at the side of the head, with the knit side facing forward. The topmost stitch (the first stitch to pick up on the Rat's right ear; the last to pick up on the left ear) should be 2 stitches from the top of the head (below).

To begin making an ear, pick up and knit 4 stitches at the side of the rat's head, with the knit side facing forward.

Turn and purl.

NEXT ROW: [K2tog] twice (2 sts).

Break yarn and draw tightly through the stitches with a tapestry needle.

ARMS/LEGS
(MAKE 2 PER BODY)

With CC, cast on 2 stitches onto one needle, and knit 12 rows of I-cord.

Break yarn and draw tightly through the stitches with a tapestry needle.

With the end still threaded on the tapestry needle, insert the I-cord horizontally through the body. For the arms, the I-cord should go in and out at the sides of the body, just to the outside of the eyes. For legs, the I-cord should go in and out at the base of the body. Pull the I-cord halfway through, so that an equal length sticks out from each side. Weave loose ends back through the I-cord and the body.

NOTE: The arms and legs are made the same length for both rats, but they appear shorter on the Fat Rat and longer on the Skinny Rat because of the difference in the Rats' circumferences.

TAIL

With CC, pick up and knit 2 stitches at the back of one of the Rats. Knit 24 rows of I-cord, then break yarn and draw tightly through the stitches with a tapestry needle.

With the end still threaded on the tapestry needle, attach the end of the tail to the other Rat with two small stitches.

FINISHING

Weave in loose ends.

The only thing a cat likes better than
a knitted rat is a pair of knitted rats!
**STUFF A LITTLE
CATNIP INSIDE**
for an extra treat for kitty.

KILLER BEES

The buzz around town is that these tough guys and their stinger switchblade are not to be messed with. Give them trouble, and the honey gets it.

BODY
(WORKED BOTTOM TO TOP)

With A, cast on 6 stitches onto 3 DPNs and join in a round.

RND 1: [Kfb] 6 times (12 sts).

RND 2: Knit.

RND 3: [Kfb, k1] 6 times (18 sts).

Switch to B.

NOTE: When switching colors, leave the old color attached until Round 16.

RND 4: Knit.

RND 5: [Kfb, k2] 6 times (24 sts).

RNDS 6–8: Switch to A, and knit 3 rounds.

RNDS 9 AND 10: Switch to B, and knit 2 rounds.

RNDS 11–13: Switch to A, and knit 3 rounds.

Switch to B.

RND 14: [K2tog, k2] 6 times (18 sts).

RND 15: Knit.

Switch to A (and break B).

RNDS 16–18: Knit 3 rounds.

Attach eyes on the last band of B, spaced 3 stitches apart.

Stuff piece.

RND 19: [K2tog, k1] 6 times (12 sts).

RND 20: [K2tog] 6 times (6 sts).

Break yarn and draw tightly through the stitches with a tapestry needle.

ARMS (MAKE 3)

With B, cast on 2 stitches, and knit 16 rows of I-cord.

Break yarn, and draw tightly through the stitches with a tapestry needle.

With the end still threaded on the tapestry needle, insert the I-cord horizontally through the sides of the body, just to the outside of the eyes. Place the bottom pair of legs just above the first B stripe; place the middle pair of legs between the first and second black stripes; and place the top pair of legs just above the second B stripe.

Pull the I-cord halfway through, so that an equal length sticks out from each side. Weave loose ends back through the I-cord and the body.

WINGS (MAKE 2)

Turn the body horizontally, with the eyes facing you. With C, pick up and knit 8 stitches, placed 4 stitches back from the arms, and spanning the 2 middle sections

TECHNIQUES

I-cord (page 138), I-cord appendages (page 22), picking up stitches (page 30)

YARN

Worsted-weight yarn in yellow, black, white, and gray

[4 MEDIUM]

Samples knit with Cascade 220, 100% wool, 3½ oz (100g), 220 yds (201m), 1 skein or less each 7827 Goldenrod (A), 8555 Black (B), 8505 White (C), 8509 Grey (D)

NEEDLES

Set of size 5 US (3.75mm) double-pointed needles

OTHER MATERIALS AND TOOLS

Size 6mm safety eyes, stuffing

FINISHED SIZE

Approx 2" (5cm) tall

GAUGE

2" (5cm) = 11 stitches and 15½ rows in stockinette stitch (knit on RS, purl on WS)

A To begin making a wing, you will pick up and knit 8 stitches at the back of the Bee's body. For the Bee's right wing, turn the body so that it faces you, with the eyes on the right.

B For the Bee's left wing, turn the body so that it faces you, with the eyes on the left.

of A. Pick up stitches so that the knit side faces forward (**A** and **B**).

You will work these stitches straight.

ROW 1: Turn and purl.
ROW 2: K1, k2tog, k2, k2tog, k1 (6 sts).
ROW 3: Purl.
ROW 4: [K2tog] 3 times (3 sts).

Break yarn and draw tightly through the stitches with a tapestry needle.

STINGER SWITCHBLADE

With C, cast on 2 stitches and knit 8 rows of I-cord. Then with D, make another 2-stitch I-cord 5 rows long. With the end threaded on a tapestry needle, thread the gray piece through the bottom end of the white one to make a knife. Attach to the Bee's arm with one small stitch.

FINISHING

Weave in loose ends

For antennae, cut a 4" strand of B, and thread it through the top of the head. Tie a knot in each end, and trim.

LITTLE MISS WIDOW

This very vogue spider knows how to accessorize, and she even creates all her fashions herself. Her lacy spiderweb headband is to die for. Don't worry, she definitely won't bite you, unless you call her a bug.

· · · · · FACTS · · · · ·

LIKES: Spinning webs, yarn, and records at spider nightclubs

HATES: Spider sweatpants

EATS: Only organic, locally harvested flies

HAUNTS: Dusty nooks in the fashion district

BODY

With A, cast on 4 stitches onto one smaller needle.

RND 1 (WORK AS AN I-CORD): [Kfb] 4 times (8 sts).

Distribute stitches onto 3 DPNs and continue to work in a round.

RND 2: [Kfb] 8 times (16 sts).

RND 3: Knit.

RND 4: [Kfb, k1] 8 times (24 sts).

RND 5: Knit.

RND 6: K3, [yo, k2] 3 times, yo, k6, [yo, k2] 3 times, yo, k3 (32 sts).

RNDS 7–12: Knit (6 rnds).

RND 13: [K2tog, k2] 8 times (24 sts).

RNDS 14 AND 15: Knit.

RND 16: [K2tog, k1] 8 times (16 sts).

RND 17: Knit.

Stuff the piece and attach the eyes, placed 3 stitches above a pair of yarn overs that are separated by 6 stitches.

RND 18: [K2tog] 8 times.

Break yarn and draw tightly through the stitches with a tapestry needle.

LEGS

With A, cast on 2 stitches onto one smaller needle.

For the front pair of legs and the back pair of legs, knit 20 rows of I-cord.

For the middle two pairs of legs, knit 18 rows of I-cord.

Break yarn and draw tightly through the stitches with a tapestry needle.

Thread the tail end of an I-cord onto the tapestry needle, and insert it horizontally through a pair of yarn overs in the body. Pull the I-cord halfway through, so that an equal length sticks out from each side. Weave loose ends back through the I-cord and the body.

BOW

With B, cast on 5 stitches onto one smaller needle to work straight.

Beginning with a purl row, work 9 rows in stockinette stitch.

Bind off with a knit row.

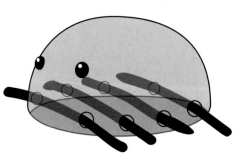
Each of the four I-cords forms two legs.

TECHNIQUES
I-cord (page 138)

YARN
Worsted-weight yarn in black, red, and white

4 MEDIUM

Samples knit with Cascade 220, 100% wool, 3½ oz (100g), 220 yds (201m), 1 skein or less each 8555 Black (A), 8414 Bright Red (B), 8505 White (C).

NEEDLES
Set of size 5 US (3.75mm) double-pointed needles, pair of size 8 US (5mm) straight needles.

OTHER MATERIALS AND TOOLS
Size 6mm safety eyes, straight pins for blocking headband, stuffing

FINISHED SIZES
Spider is approx 1½" (3.8cm) tall

Headband sizes (measured from top of ear to top of ear)

Child (9–11"), Adult (11–14")

GAUGE FOR SMALLER NEEDLES
2" (5cm) = 11 stitches and 15½ rows in stockinette stitch (knit on RS, purl on WS)

GAUGE FOR LARGER NEEDLES
2" (5cm) = 9 stitches and 11 rows in stockinette stitch (knit on RS, purl on WS)

Cut a strand of yarn about 5" (12.5cm) long, and tie it tightly around the middle of the flat piece you just finished, knotting it in back on the purl side. Tightly wrap loose ends around the piece a few more times and knot again in the same place. Use the loose ends to stitch to the spider's head.

HEADBAND

With C, cast on 3 stitches onto one smaller needle.

For child size, knit a 7" (18cm) long I-cord; for adult size, knit a 9" (23cm) long I-cord.

You will continue to work the piece straight.

HEADBAND INCREASE

ROW 1: Kfb, k1, kfb (5 sts).
ROW 2: Purl.
ROW 3: K1, kfb, k to last 2 sts, kfb, k1 (7 sts).
ROW 4: Purl.
ROW 5: Work same as Row 3 (9 sts).
ROW 6: Purl.
ROW 7: Work same as Row 3 (11 sts).
ROW 8: Purl.

Switch to larger needles.

LACE PATTERN

ROW 1: K1, [yo, k2tog] twice, k1, [k2tog, yo] twice, k1.
ROW 2: Purl.
ROW 3: K1, [k2tog, yo] twice, k1, [yo, k2tog] twice, k1.
ROW 4: Purl.

Repeat these 4 rows of lace pattern until you have a total of 13 repeats for child size, or 16 total repeats for adult size.

Work Rows 1 and 2 once more.

HEADBAND DECREASE

Switch to smaller needles.
ROW 1: K1, k2tog, k to last 3 sts, k2tog, k1 (9 sts).
ROW 2: Purl.
ROW 3: Work same as Row 1 (7 sts).
ROW 4: Purl.

ROW 5: Work same as Row 1 (5 sts).
ROW 6: Purl.
ROW 7: K2tog, k1, k2tog (3 sts).

With these 3 stitches, for child size, knit a 7" (18cm) long I-cord; for adult size, knit a 9" (23cm) long I-cord.

Break yarn and draw tightly through the stitches with a tapestry needle.

FINISHING

Block the headband by dampening it, then gently stretching it and pinning it onto a flat surface like an ironing board to dry. To make points in the "web," gently pull out every other yarn over on the sides of the piece and pin in place (below).

Attach the spider to the side of the headband with a few stitches on the underside of the spider.

Weave in loose ends.

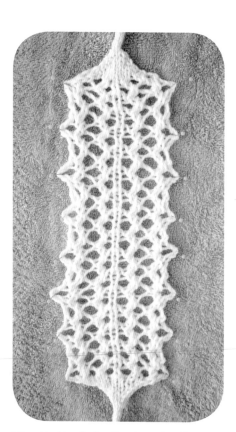

When blocking the headband, gently pull out every other yarn over on the edges of the piece.

MAMA BEAR CAVE

Don't get too close to this protective mom—her cubs may look super-cuddly, but those sharp teeth say stay back! Let's just hope she doesn't get the hiccups and swallow her brood by accident.

······· F A C T S ·······

LIKES: Stalactites
HATES: Stalagmites
EATS: Cub chasers
HAUNTS: Parent Bear Association meetings

Mama Bear
BODY
BASE

Using a provisional cast-on with waste yarn and a crochet hook, cast on 24 stitches of A onto the circular needle to work straight.

ROW 1 AND ALL ODD-NUMBERED ROWS: Purl.

ROW 2: K1, [kfb] twice, k to last 3 sts, [kfb] twice, k1 (28 sts).

ROW 4: Work same as Row 2 (32 sts).

ROW 6: Work same as Row 2 (36 sts).

ROW 8: K1, kfb, k to last 2 sts, kfb, k1 (38 sts).

ROW 10: Work same as Row 8 (40 sts).

ROW 12: Work same as Row 8 (42 sts).

ROWS 14–24: Beginning with a knit row, work 12 rows in stockinette stitch.

ROW 26: K1, k2tog, k to last 3 sts, k2tog, k1 (40 sts).

ROW 28: Work same as Row 26 (38 sts).

ROW 30: Work same as Row 26 (36 sts).

ROW 32: K1, [k2tog] twice, k to last 5 sts, [k2tog] twice, k1 (32 sts).

ROW 34: Work same as Row 32 (28 sts).

ROW 36: Work same as Row 32 (24 sts).

Work Row 37, then bind off on the right side until there is one stitch remaining on the needle in your right hand. You will leave that stitch on the needle as you pick up stitches to form the sides of the cave.

SIDES

Rotate the piece clockwise, and pick up and knit 23 stitches along the side of the piece. Undo and remove the waste yarn, and place these 24 stitches on a DPN, then knit onto the circular needle. Continue to rotate the piece, and pick up and knit 24 stitches along the next side. You will now have 72 stitches on your needle, attached in a U shape to the base. You will work these stitches straight to form the cave mouth (page 82).

ROWS 1–5: Turn and, beginning with a purl row, work 5 rows in stockinette stitch.

ROW 6: K1, kfb, k to last 2 sts, kfb, k1 (74 sts).

ROW 7: Purl.

ROW 8: Work same as Row 6 (76 sts).

ROW 9: Purl.

ROW 10: K1, [kfb] twice, k to last 3 sts, [kfb] twice, k1 (80 sts).

ROW 11: Purl.

ROW 12: Work same as Row 10 (84 sts).

Instead of turning for a purl row, you will now create the top of the cave mouth and then join the stitches in a round. Place marker for the beginning of the round.

RND 13: Cast on 12 stitches using the backward loop method, knit to the end (96 sts).

RND 14: Knit.

TECHNIQUES

Provisional cast-on (page 137), backward loop cast-on (page 136), mattress stitch (page 23), I-cord (page 138), I-cord appendages (page 22), attaching hair (page 33)

YARN

Bulky yarn in 2 shades of brown, black, gray, and a small amount of green

5 BULKY

Samples knit with Cascade 128 Superwash, 100% wool, 3½ oz (100g), 128 yds (117m), 2 skeins 1920 Pumpkin Spice (A), 1 skein or less each 1982 Harvest Orange (B), 815 Black (C), 1946 Silver (D), 841 Moss (E)

NEEDLES

Set of size 8 US (5mm) double-pointed needles, 16" (40.5cm) size 8 US circular needle

OTHER MATERIALS AND TOOLS

Waste yarn and crochet hook, size 15mm safety eyes, straight pins, stuffing

FINISHED SIZE

Approx 7½" (19cm) tall

GAUGE

2" (5cm) = 8 stitches and 12 rows in stockinette stitch (knit on RS, purl on WS)

NOTE: The circular needle can be replaced by double-pointed needles, and vice versa, if you use a long circular needle and the magic loop method for smaller pieces.

RND 15: [K2tog, k10] 8 times (88 sts).

RNDS 16 AND 17: Knit.

RND 18: [K2tog, k9] 8 times (80 sts).

RNDS 19 AND 20: Knit.

RND 21: [K2tog, k8] 8 times (72 sts).

RNDS 22 AND 23: Knit.

RND 24: [K2tog, k7] 8 times (64 sts).

RNDS 25 AND 26: Knit.

RND 27: [K2tog, k6] 8 times (56 sts).

Transfer stitches to 3 DPNs and continue to work in a round.

RND 28 AND ALL EVEN-NUMBERED RNDS THROUGH RND 36: Knit.

RND 29: [K2tog, k5] 8 times (48 sts).

RND 31: [K2tog, k4] 8 times (40 sts).

RND 33: [K2tog, k3] 8 times (32 sts).

RND 35: [K2tog, k2] 8 times (24 sts).

RND 37: [K2tog, k1] 8 times (16 sts).

RND 38: [K2tog] 8 times (8 sts).

Break yarn and draw tightly through the stitches with a tapestry needle.

CAVE LINING

With C, cast on 48 stitches onto 3 DPNs and join in a round.

RNDS 1–18: Knit.

RND 19: [K2tog, k6] 6 times (42 sts).

RND 20 AND ALL EVEN-NUMBERED RNDS THROUGH RND 28: Knit.

RND 21: [K2tog, k5] 6 times (36 sts).

RND 23: [K2tog, k4] 6 times (30 sts).

RND 25: [K2tog, k3] 6 times (24 sts).

RND 27: [K2tog, k2] 6 times (18 sts).

RND 29: [K2tog, k1] 6 times (12 sts).

RND 30: [K2tog] 6 times (6 sts).

Break yarn and draw tightly through the stitches with a tapestry needle.

TEETH (MAKE 4)

With D, cast on 9 stitches onto 3 DPNs and join in a round.

RNDS 1–3: Knit.

RND 4: [K2tog, k1] 3 times (6 sts).

RNDS 5 AND 6: Knit.

Break yarn and draw tightly through the stitches with a tapestry needle.

Ⓐ To begin forming the sides of the body, you will pick up and knit stitches around the piece, leaving a space where the mouth will go.

EARS (MAKE 2)

With A, cast on 16 stitches onto 3 DPNs and join in a round.

RNDS 1–3: Knit.

RND 4: K2tog, k4, [k2tog] twice, k4, k2tog (12 sts).

RND 5: Knit.

RND 6: K2tog, k2, [k2tog] twice, k2, k2tog (8 sts).

Break yarn and draw tightly through the stitches with a tapestry needle.

PAWS (MAKE 2)

With A, cast on 4 stitches onto one DPN, leaving a tail for seaming.

RND 1 (WORK AS AN I-CORD): [Kfb] 4 times (8 sts).

Distribute stitches onto 3 DPNs to continue to work in a round.

RND 2: [Kfb] 8 times (16 sts).

RND 3: Knit.

RND 4: Kfb, k6, [kfb] twice, k6, kfb (20 sts).

RNDS 5–12: Knit (8 rnds).

RND 13: [K2tog] twice, k2, [k2tog] 4 times, k2 [k2tog] twice (12 sts)

RND 14: Knit.

Stuff the piece.

RND 15: K2tog, k2, [k2tog] twice, k2, k2tog (8 sts).

Break yarn and draw tightly through the stitches with a tapestry needle.

CLAWS (MAKE 4)

With D, cast on 2 stitches onto one DPN, and knit 10 rows of I-cord.

Break yarn and draw tightly through the stitches with a tapestry needle.

With the end still threaded on the tapestry needle, insert the I-cord through the closed-up end of the paw. (Use one I-cord to make the first and second claws on a paw, and another to make the third and fourth claws.) Pull the I-cord halfway through, so that an equal length sticks out from each side. Weave loose ends back through the I-cord and the paw.

B When attaching the cave lining to the mouth, pin the teeth in place, and insert the tapestry needle straight through the teeth when you come to them.

C After inserting the tapestry needle through a tooth, continue seaming using mattress stitch, as if the tooth weren't there.

FINISHING MAMA BEAR

Attach eyes to the body, placed about 7 stitches up from the cave hole, and spaced about 12 stitches apart.

Leaving teeth unstuffed, pin their cast-on edges to the edges of the cave mouth, with the top two teeth spaced 2 stitches apart and the bottom teeth spaced just outside the top teeth.

Insert the cave lining into the mouth, with the purl sides of the body and the lining facing each other, and align the cast-on and bound-off edges of the mouth with the cast-on edge of the lining. Begin seaming the edges together using mattress stitch, starting in one corner of the mouth.

When you come to a tooth, make your stitches go straight through the tooth with each stitch, while continuing to use mattress stitch on the mouth and lining. When you pull the seam tight, the teeth will be neatly integrated into the seam (**B** and **C**).

Stuff the piece before closing up the seam, making sure to fill the shape out, while still allowing the lining to be concave within the body.

Flatten the ears and, without stuffing them, attach their cast-on edges to the top of the body using mattress stitch, each placed 8 stitches from top.

Attach the paws to the body, a few stitches outside the mouth.

With C, embroider the nose with 4 horizontal stitches (2 longer on top and 2 shorter on bottom) placed 4 stitches above the mouth.

For grass, cut 3 strands of E about 4" (10cm) in length. Insert a crochet hook under a stitch on the body, fold a strand of yarn in half, and with the crochet hook pull it through the stitch. Tuck the loose ends of the yarn through the loop that you've pulled through, and pull tightly. Trim to desired length.

Weave in loose ends.

Cub

With B, cast on 6 stitches onto 3 DPNs and join in a round.

RND 1: [Kfb] 6 times (12 sts).

RND 2: Knit.

RND 3: [Kfb, k1] twice, yo, k4, yo, [kfb k1] twice (18 sts).

RNDS 4–9: Knit (6 rnds).

RND 10: K7, yo, [k2tog] twice, yo, k7 (18 sts).

RNDS 11 AND 12: Knit.

RND 13: [K2tog, k1] 6 times (12 sts).

RND 14: Knit.

Stuff the piece.

RND 15: [K2tog] 6 times (6 sts).

Break yarn and draw tightly through the stitches with a tapestry needle.

With B, cast on 4 stitches onto one needle.

Knit an I-cord for 10 rows.

Break yarn and draw tightly through the stitches with a tapestry needle.

With the end still threaded on the tapestry needle, insert the I-cord back to front through the yarn-over holes in the body. (One I-cord will form one back leg and one front leg.) Pull the I-cord halfway through so that an equal length sticks out from each yarn-over hole. Weave loose ends back through the I-cord and the body.

With C, embroider eyes with 2 stitches for each, placed about 4 stitches back from the closed-up end of the Cub, and spaced 4 stitches apart. Embroider the nose in the middle of the face between the eyes with 3 horizontal stitches.

For ears, cut a 12" (30.48cm) strand of B, and embroider 4 stitches over the same place behind each eye. Embroider the tail at the cast-on end of the Cub in the same way.

Weave in loose ends.

A sheltered childhood
has never been so
DANGEROUS.

CREEPY NEW SPECIES

Did you know that scientists are discovering thousands of new creatures each year? These extra-weird ones are so new, they're still waiting to be found. (It might be a long wait.)

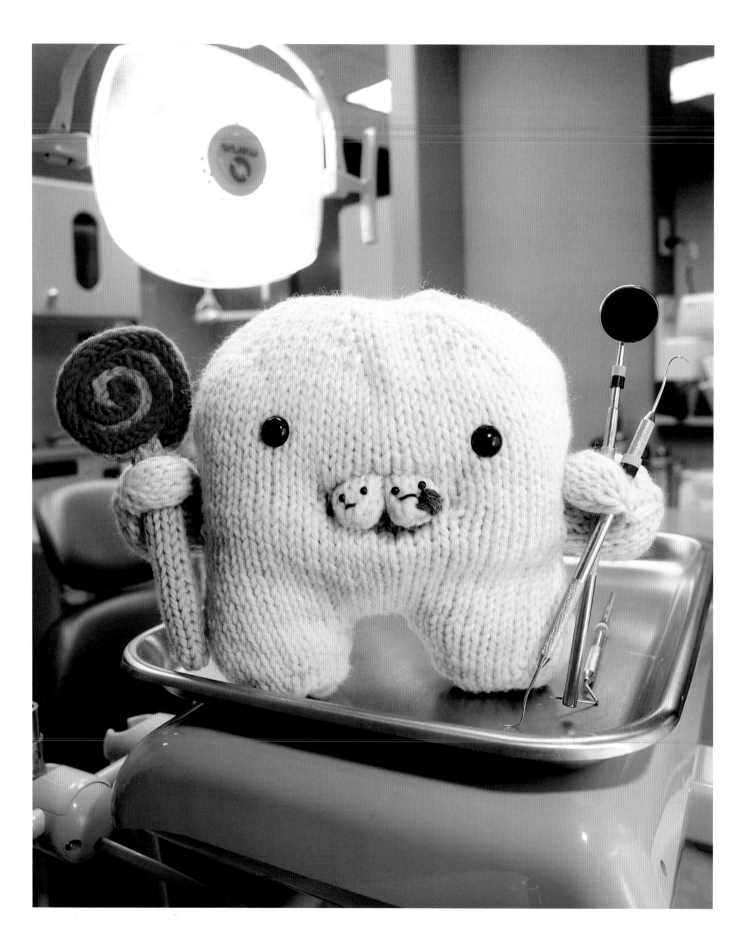

SOUR TOOTH

Armed with a tempting lollipop, this huggable molar will try to trick you into getting cavities! If you're lucky enough to lose a tooth, though, he'll stash it away in his mouth and turn it into delicious cash.

FACTS

LIKES: Gap-toothed grins
HATES: His nemesis, Dr. Floss (not pictured)
EATS: Candy and molars
HAUNTS: Sweet shops and dentists' offices

TECHNIQUES
Joining pieces (page 28), backward loop cast-on (page 136), Kitchener stitch (page 140), mattress stitch (page 23), I-cord (page 138)

YARN
Bulky yarn in 4 colors

(5 BULKY)

Samples knit with Cascade 128 Superwash, 100% wool, 3½ oz (100g), 128 yds (117m), 1 skein or less each 817 Ecru (A), 901 Cotton Candy (B), 1964 Cerise (C), 821 Daffodil (E)

Small amount of black fingering-weight yarn (for tiny teeth's mouths)

Small amount of gray worsted-weight yarn (for tiny tooth's cavity)

NEEDLES
Set of size 8 US (5.0 mm) double-pointed needles, 16" size 8 US (5.0 mm) circular needle

OTHER MATERIALS AND TOOLS
1 set size 12mm safety eyes, 2 sets size 3mm bead eyes, straight pins, stuffing

FINISHED SIZE
Approx 7½" (19cm) tall

GAUGE
2" (5cm) = 8 stitches and 12 rows in stockinette stitch (knit on RS, purl on WS)

NOTE: The circular needle can be replaced by double-pointed needles, and vice versa, if you use a long circular needle and the magic loop method.

BODY

LEGS

With A, cast on 6 stitches onto 3 needles and join in a round.

RND 1: [Kfb] 6 times (12 sts).

RND 2: [Kfb, k1] 6 times (18 sts).

RNDS 3 AND 4: Knit.

RND 5: [Kfb, k2] 6 times (24 sts).

RNDS 6 AND 7: Knit.

RND 8: [Kfb, k3] 6 times (30 sts).

RNDS 9 AND 10: Knit.

Break yarn. Divide stitches onto 2 spare needles, and set aside.

Repeat Rounds 1–10 above to make another leg, without breaking yarn. Divide these stitches onto 2 needles.

JOIN LEGS

Distribute the stitches of both legs onto 2 needles, with the first 15 stitches of each leg on one needle and the last 15 stitches of each leg on another. Hold the needles

A To get ready to join the legs together, divide the stitches of each leg and place them onto two needles, then transfer them in order onto a circular needle.

so that the working yarn is attached to the rightmost stitch on the back needle. Next, pick up the circular needle, and slip the stitches onto it, beginning with the rightmost stitch on the front needle. When you've transfered all 30 stitches from the front needle, continue in order with the leftmost stitch on the back needle, so that the last stitch you transfer has the working yarn attached (**A**).

You will now work the piece in the round, joining the two legs together.

K15, cast on 4 stitches using the backward loop method, k30, cast on 4 more stitches using the backward loop method, k15 (68 sts).

SHAPE BODY

RND 1: K1, k2tog, k28, k2tog, k1, pm, k1, k2tog, k to last 3 sts, k2tog, k1 (64 sts).

RNDS 2 AND 3: Knit.

RND 4: K1, k2tog, k to 3 sts before marker, k2tog, k1, sm, k1, k2tog, k to last 3 sts, k2tog, k1 (60 sts).

RNDS 5 AND 6: Knit.

RND 7: Work same as Rnd 4 (56 sts).

RNDS 8–11: Knit.

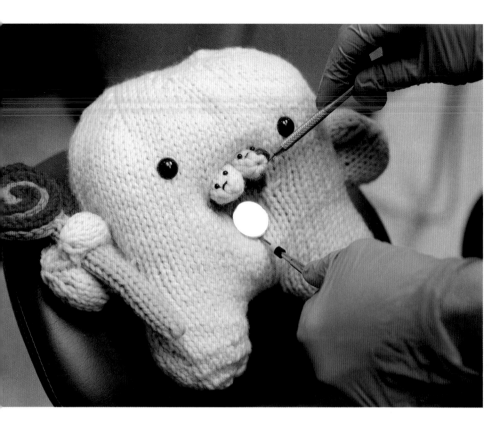

RND 12: [K2tog] twice, k2, [k2tog] 4 times, k2, [k2tog] twice (12 sts).

RND 13: Knit.

Stuff piece.

RND 14: [K2tog] 6 times (6 sts).

Break yarn and draw tightly through the stitches with a tapestry needle.

THUMB

With A, pick up and knit 3 stitches along Rnd 4 on the hand piece, then flip the piece around and pick up and knit 3 more stitches parallel to the first 3 (**B**). Distribute 6 stitches onto 3 needles to work in a round.

RND 1: Knit.

RND 2: [Kfb, k1] 3 times (9 sts).

RNDS 3–5: Knit.

RND 6: [K2tog, k1] 3 times (6 sts).

Insert a small amount of stuffing, then break yarn and draw tightly through the stitches with a tapestry needle.

With the tail still threaded on the tapestry needle, stitch the tip of the thumb down onto the hand at an angle, so the thumb is pointing inward and toward the tip of the hand. This will give you a loop to insert candy or other objects into. Make the thumbs of the each hand lie in an opposite direction, so that they mirror each other.

RND 12: K1, kfb, k to 2 sts before marker, kfb, k1, sm, k1, kfb, k to last 2 sts, kfb, k1 (60 sts).

RNDS 13 AND 14: Knit.

RND 15: Work same as Rnd 12 (64 sts).

RND 16: K13, BO 6 sts (begin binding off with 14th and 15th sts), k to end (58 sts).

RND 17: K13, cast on 6 sts using the backward loop method, k to end (64 sts).

RND 18: Work same as Rnd 12 (68 sts).

RNDS 19 AND 20: Knit.

RND 21: Work same as Rnd 12 (72 sts).

RNDS 22–29: Knit (8 rnds).

RND 30: [K2tog, k7] 8 times (64 sts).

ODD-NUMBERED RNDS 31–39: Knit.

RND 32: [K2tog, k6] 8 times (56 sts).

RND 34: [K2tog, k5] 8 times (48 sts).

RND 36: [K2tog, k4] 8 times (40 sts).

RND 38: [K2tog, k3] 8 times (32 sts).

RND 40: [K2tog] twice, k8, [k2tog] twice, sm, [k2tog] twice, k8, [k2tog] twice (24 sts).

Divide stitches onto either end of the needle, and bind off using Kitchener stitch.

MOUTH POCKET

With B, cast on 14 stitches onto 3 needles and join in a round.

Knit 12 rounds.

Divide stitches onto 2 needles and bind off using Kitchener stitch.

TINY TEETH (MAKE 2)

With A, cast on 8 stitches onto 3 needles and join in a round.

Knit 4 rounds.

Break yarn and draw tightly through the stitches with a tapestry needle.

ARMS (MAKE 2)

With A, cast on 6 stitches onto 3 needles, leaving a tail for seaming, and join in a round.

RND 1: [Kfb] 6 times (12 sts).

RNDS 2–4: Knit.

RND 5: Kfb, k4, [kfb] twice, k4, kfb (16 sts).

RND 6: Knit.

RND 7: Kfb, k6, [kfb] twice, k6, kfb (20 sts).

RND 8–11: Knit.

B To begin making a thumb, pick up and knit 6 stitches in two parallel groups of 3.

FINISHING TOOTH

Attach eyes to the body about 4 stitches above the mouth hole and spaced 12 stitches apart. Stuff the main piece through the mouth hole and the gap left between the legs.

Seam the gap between the legs using mattress stitch.

Turn the mouth pocket purl side out, and insert it into the mouth hole, aligning the cast-on edge of the pocket with the cast-on/bound-off edges of the hole. With A, begin seaming the edges together using mattress stitch, starting with the bottom of the mouth. When you reach the top of the mouth, stuff the two tiny teeth and insert their cast-on edges between the open edges of the pocket and the hole. Pin the teeth to the edge of the hole so that they will stay in place as you seam.

Continue seaming the mouth, and when you come to the teeth, make your stitches go straight through the teeth with each stitch, while continuing to use mattress stitch on the mouth pocket and hole, as you had been. When you pull the seam tightly, the teeth will be neatly integrated into the seam (**C** and **D**).

Attach arms at the sides of the body using mattress stitch, with thumbs facing up and pointing forward.

Sew bead eyes onto the tiny teeth, and embroider mouths with one stitch of fingering-weight yarn for each.

With gray worsted-weight yarn, embroider a cavity onto one of the tiny teeth with several parallel stitches.

Weave in loose ends.

LOLLIPOP

Cast on 2 stitches of B and 2 stitches of C side by side onto one needle.

Slide the 4 stitches to the right end of the needle, and knit the first 2 stitches of B as an I-cord. Drop B, and knit the first stitch of C. Before knitting the second stitch of C, wrap B around C once at back to join the 2 colors. Once you have knitted the second stitch of C, slide stitches down to the right end of the needle again, and repeat this pattern. You will end up with two I-cords joined together.

Continue as established until the I-cord measures approximately 12" (30.5cm) long. Break yarns, leaving the long tails

for seaming, and draw both tails tightly through the stitches with a tapestry needle.

Coil the piece tightly, with the tails on the outer edge, and lay it on a flat surface. Using the tail ends individually, make long, loose, horizontal stitches that go through each layer of the I-cord, until the piece is solid and won't uncoil (**E**).

STICK

With D, cast on 6 stitches onto 3 needles, leaving a tail for seaming, and join to work in a round.

Knit 20 rounds, stuffing the piece as you go.

Break yarn and draw tightly through the stitches with a tapestry needle.

Attach the cast-on edge of the stick to the lollipop coil, using mattress stitch.

Weave in loose ends.

C When attaching the mouth pocket into the mouth, pin the tiny teeth in place, and insert the tapestry needle straight through the tiny teeth when you come to them.

D After inserting the tapestry needle through a tiny tooth, continue seaming using mattress stitch, as if the tooth weren't there.

E Coil the lollipop I-cords together tightly, lay the coiled I-cords on a flat surface, and sew them together with stitches that go through all the layers.

HURLY-BURLY

Grab the sawdust—something's on its way up!

This self-regurgitating pair of tummy-turners have made motion sickness into a way of life. It must have been something they ate.

· · · · · · F A C T S · · · · · ·

LIKES: Spinning themselves silly

HATES: Polite company

EATS: Nothing, their mouths are already too full!

HAUNTS: Amusement parks and tire swings

BODIES

With A, cast on 4 stitches onto one needle.

RND 1 (WORK AS AN I-CORD): [Kfb] 4 times (8 sts).

Distribute stitches onto 4 needles and continue to work in a round.

RND 2: [Kfb] 8 times (16 sts).
Switch to B.

RND 3: Knit.

RND 4: [Kfb, k1] 8 times (24 sts).
Switch to A.

RND 5: Knit.

RND 6: [Kfb, k2] 8 times (32 sts).

Continue to switch colors every 2 rounds, and increase 8 stitches every other round (working one more stitch after each kfb in the round), until there are 104 stitches on your needles. You should have just finished working 2 rounds with B.

RNDS 25 AND 26: Switch to A, and knit 2 rounds.

RNDS 27 AND 28: Switch to B, and knit 2 rounds.

RNDS 29 AND 30: Switch to A, and knit 2 rounds.

RNDS 31 AND 32: Switch to B, and knit 2 rounds.

RND 33: Switch to A, and knit 1 round.

RND 34: [K2tog, k11] 8 times (96 sts).
Switch to B.

RND 35: Knit.

RND 36: [K2tog, k10] 8 times (88 sts).
Switch to A.

RND 37: Knit.

RND 38: [K2tog, k9] 8 times (80 sts).

Continue to switch colors every 2 rounds, and decrease 8 stitches every other round (working one less knitted stitch after each k2tog in the round), until there are 24 stitches on your needles. You should have just finished working 2 rounds with B.

Switch to C.

RND 53: Knit.

RND 54: [Kfb, k2] 8 times (32 sts).

RND 55: Knit

RND 56: [Kfb, k3] 8 times (40 sts).
Switch to D.

RND 57: Knit.

RND 58: [Kfb, k4] (48 sts).

RND 59: Knit.

RND 60: [Kfb, k5] (56 sts).

Continue to switch colors every 4 rounds, and increase 8 stitches every other round (working one more knitted stitch after each kfb in the round), until there are 104 stitches on your needles. You should have just finished working 4 rounds with C.

RNDS 73–76: Switch to D, and knit 4 rounds.

RNDS 77–80: Switch to C, and knit 4 rounds.

Switch to D.

RND 81: Knit.

RND 82: [K2tog, k11] 8 times (96 sts).

RND 83: Knit.

TECHNIQUES

Picking up stitches (page 30), I-cord (page 138), attaching hair (page 33)

YARN

Worsted-weight yarn in 4 colors

4 MEDIUM

Samples knit with Cascade 220, 100% wool, 3½ oz (100g), 220 yds (201m), 1 skein each 7808 Purple Hyacinth (A), 8912 Lilac Mist (B), 9542 Blaze (C), 7828 Neon Yellow (D)

NEEDLES

Set of five 7" (18cm) size 5 US (3.75mm) double-pointed needles

OTHER MATERIALS AND TOOLS

2 sets size 12mm safety eyes, crochet hook (for attaching hair), stuffing

FINISHED SIZE

Approx 5" (12.5cm) tall

GAUGE

2" (5cm) = 11 stitches and 15½ rows in stockinette stitch (knit on RS, purl on WS)

NOTES: When working the A/B half of the body, carry the two yarns up between color changes until you reach the C/D half. Do the same with the C and D yarns.

When switching colors, wrap the old color once around the new color after knitting one stitch with the new color.

A The bodies are knitted as one piece, joined at the mouth.

B Before closing up the bodies, stuff one inside the other and stuff through the opening at the back.

RND 84: [K2tog, k10] 8 times (88 sts).
Switch to C.

RND 85: Knit.

RND 86: [K2tog, k9] 8 times (80 sts).

RND 87: Knit.

RND 88: [K2tog, k8] 8 times (72 sts).

RNDS 89 TO 100: Continue to switch colors every 4 rounds, and decrease 8 stitches every other round (working one less knitted stitch after each k2tog in the round), until there are 24 stitches on your needles. You should have just finished working 4 rounds with D.

Attach eyes as shown, keeping in mind that the place where the color combination changes will become the mouth for both bodies. The spacing of the eyes can vary, and don't worry about aligning the two sets of eyes with each other (**A**).

Stuff the A/B portion of the piece into the C/D portion. Insert stuffing into the piece through the opening at the back of the C/D section. Stuff it enough so that the body is filled out, but without overstuffing it so much that the A/B portion won't comfortably fit inside (**B**).

Switch to C.

RND 101: Knit.

RND 102: [K2tog, k1] 8 times (16 sts).

RND 103: [K2tog] 8 times (8 sts).

Break yarn, and draw tightly through the stitches with a tapestry needle.

ARMS/LEGS

NOTE: Work each arm/leg while the corresponding body is on the outside, flipping the piece inside out to reveal the other body when you are ready to make the appendages for it.

With B (or D) pick up and knit 4 stitches on the body (**C** page 96). Placement can vary, as shown in the samples.

Knit 10 rows of I-cord.

Switch to A (or C).

Knit one row of I-cord.

RND 12 (WORK AS AN I-CORD): [Kfb] 4 times (8 sts).

C To make an arm or a leg, begin by picking up and knitting 4 stitches at the front side of the body.

Distribute stitches onto 3 DPNs and continue to work in a round.

RND 13: [Kfb] 8 times (16 sts).

RNDS 14–19: Knit (6 rnds).

RND 20: [K2tog] 8 times (8 sts).

Stuff the ball portion of the piece, then break the yarn, and draw tightly through the stitches with a tapestry needle.

FINISHING

Weave in loose ends.

For hair, cut a few strands of yarn about 4" (10cm) long. Insert a crochet hook under a stitch, and use it to pull through a strand of yarn that you've folded in half. Tuck the loose ends of the yarn through the loop that you've pulled through, and pull tightly.

For pigtails, use a strand of contrasting-colored yarn to tie the yarn hair in place.

To turn Hurly-Burly inside out, hold the mouth open with your thumbs, and push on the back with your fingers (**D**).

D To turn Hurly-Burly inside out, hold the mouth open with your thumbs, and push on the back with your fingers.

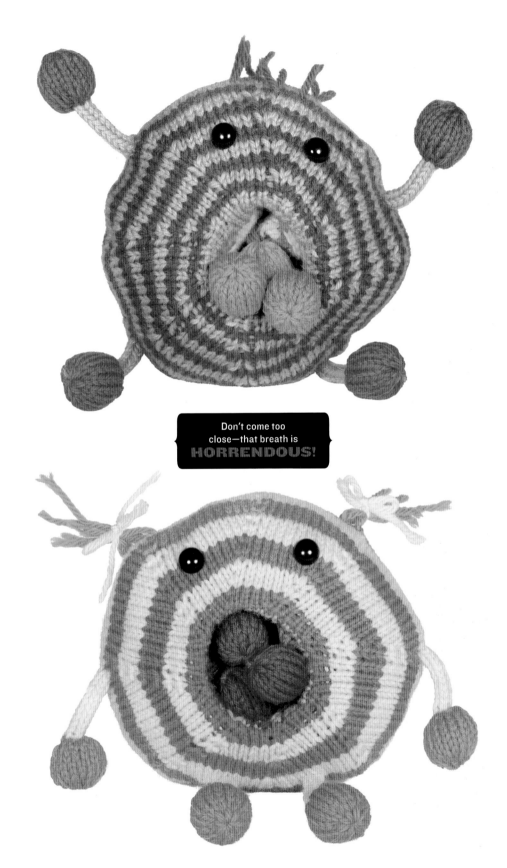

Don't come too close—that breath is HORRENDOUS!

MINITAURS

Quietly existing on a tiny island off the coast of Crete
for a few thousand years, these bullish little beasts have evolved to be even worse at solving puzzles than their mythical ancestor. It's a good thing they can't find their way off the island, because they've also evolved the ability to gore you with their tiny little horns.

BODY

LEGS

With A, cast on 4 stitches onto one needle.

Knit 3 rows of I-cord, then break the yarn and set it aside on a spare needle.

Make a second leg the same way as the first, without breaking the yarn.

JOIN LEGS

Distribute the stitches of both legs onto 2 needles, with the first 2 stitches of each leg on one needle and the second 2 stitches of each leg on another. Hold the needles so that the working yarn is attached to the rightmost stitch on the back needle.

Knit one round, starting with the needle in front, then flipping needles around and continuing on with the back needle.

Distribute 8 stitches onto 3 needles to continue to work in a round.

SHAPE BODY

RND 1: [Kfb] 8 times (16 sts).
RND 2: Knit.

Switch to B.

RNDS 3–5: Knit.
RND 6: [Kfb, k3] 4 times (20 sts).
RNDS 7–10: Knit.
RND 11: [Kfb, k4] 4 times (24 sts).

RNDS 12–15: Knit.
RND 16: [K2tog, k1] 8 times (16 sts).
RND 17: Knit.

Stuff the piece before continuing.

RND 18: [K2tog] 8 times (8 sts).

Break yarn and draw tightly through the stitches with a tapestry needle.

FEATURES

With C, embroider the eyes with 2 stitches for each one, placed 6 stitches down from the top of the head and spaced 4 stitches apart.

With C, embroider the mouth with 3 longer horizontal stitches, placed 4 stitches down from the eyes.

ARMS

With B, cast on 2 stitches onto one needle.

Knit 12 rows of I-cord, then break yarn and draw tightly through the stitches with a tapestry needle.

With the end still threaded on a tapestry needle, insert the I-cord through the body, going in and coming out at the sides of the body, just above the color change. Pull the I-cord halfway through, so that an equal length sticks out from each side. Weave loose ends back through the I-cord and the body.

HORNS

With A, cast on 2 stitches onto one needle.

Knit 18 rows of I-cord, then break yarn and draw tightly through the stitches with a tapestry needle.

With the end still threaded on a tapestry needle, insert the I-cord through the body, going in and coming out at the sides of the head, 3 stitches down from the top. Weave loose ends back through the I-cord and the body, pinching the horns into an upturned shape as you do so.

FINISHING

Weave in loose ends.

For hair, cut 2 strands of B about 2" (5cm) long. Insert a crochet hook under a stitch at the top of the head, and use it to pull through a strand of yarn that you've folded in half. Tuck the loose ends of the yarn through the loop that you've pulled through, and pull tightly. Repeat with the second piece.

Use the tip of a pair of sharp scissors to separate the individual strands of hair for a shaggy look. Trim to desired length.

WATCH YOUR STEP——
these tiny toros are known for
stubbing toes!

FLATSO

Here's a crash diet gone bad: The mysterious Flatso
is so svelte that he is nearly invisible when seen in profile. He may be lurking in your bookshelf or under your couch cushions, but don't be alarmed—you can tame this beast by feeding him an iPad.

F A C T S

LIKES: Always winning at limbo
HATES: Pleats (he thinks they make him look fat!)
EATS: Data is his favorite food, but he'll also eat change lost in the couch
HAUNTS: Cozy corners and the bottom of backpacks

To make a neat cuff, transfer the provisional cast-on stitches onto a spare circular needle, bring the spare needle up behind the working needle, and knit each stitch in the round together with the corresponding stitch on the spare needle.

TECHNIQUES

Provisional cast-on (page 137), backward loop cast-on (page 136), Kitchener stitch (page 140), mattress stitch (page 23)

YARN

Bulky yarn in 2 colors plus a small amount of black

Samples knit with Cascade 128 Superwash, 100% wool, 3½ oz (100g), 128 yds (117m), 1 skein or less each 821 Daffodil (A), 1964 Cerise (B), 8555 Black (C)

NEEDLES

16" (40.5cm) size 8 US (5mm) circular needle, spare circular needle (any length, size 8 US or smaller), set of size 8 US (5mm) double-pointed needles

OTHER MATERIALS AND TOOLS

Crochet hook and waste yarn, ¾" (2cm) button, stuffing

FINISHED SIZE

Approx 10½" (26.5cm) long (not including tongue) and 6¾" (17cm) wide

GAUGE

2" (5cm) = 8 stitches and 12 rows in stockinette stitch (knit on RS, purl on WS)

NOTE

Checking gauge is recommended if you want to make sure an iPad or other device will fit into Flatso.

BODY

With waste yarn and a crochet hook, provisionally cast on 58 stitches onto a size 8 US circular needle, and join to work in a round, taking care not to twist the stitches.

RNDS 1–8: Knit.

RND 9: Undo waste yarn, and slip the provisional cast-on stitches onto a spare circular needle. Bring that needle up behind your working needle, and with A knit the two together, knitting each stitch from the working needle together with the corresponding stitch on the spare needle. This will form Flatso's mouth and makes a trim-looking cuff for the iPad carrier.

RNDS 10–37: Knit (28 rnds).

Switch to B (without breaking A).

RNDS 38 AND 39: Knit.

For Rnds 40–63, repeat the color pattern of Rnds 1–6 below 4 times total (24 rnds).

RNDS 1 AND 2: [K1B, k1A] to end.

RND 3: Knit in B.

RNDS 4 AND 5: [K1A, k1B] to end.

RND 6: Knit in B.

Switch to B, and break A.

RND 64: Knit.

Divide stitches evenly onto either end of the needle, and bind off using Kitchener stitch.

ARMS/LEGS (MAKE 4)

With A, cast on 14 stitches onto 3 DPNs and join in a round.

Knit 9 rounds.

Divide stitches onto 2 needles, and bind off using Kitchener stitch.

Lay piece flat, and without stuffing it, seam the open cast-on edges using mattress stitch.

Attach the button where the tongue's buttonhole sits on the underside.

EARS (MAKE 2)

With A, cast on 12 stitches onto 3 DPNs and join in a round.

RNDS 1–3: Knit.

RND 4: K2tog, k2, [k2tog] twice, k2, k2tog (8 sts).

RNDS 5–7: Knit.

RND 8: [K2tog] 4 times (4 sts).

Break yarn, and draw tightly through the stitches with a tapestry needle.

Lay the piece flat and, without stuffing it, seam the open cast-on edges using mattress stitch.

TONGUE

With B, cast on 16 stitches onto 3 DPNs and join in a round.

RNDS 1–14: Knit.

RND 15: K3, BO 2 sts (begin binding off with 4th and 5th sts), k5, BO 2 sts, k2 (12 sts).

NOTE: After Rnd 15, you will have two groups of 6 stitches separated by bound-off stitches.

RND 16: K3, cast on 2 sts using the backward loop method, k6, cast on 2 stitches using the backward loop method, k3 (16 sts).

RNDS 17 AND 18: Knit.

RND 19: K2tog, k4, [k2tog] twice, k4, k2tog (12 sts).

RND 20: Knit.

RND 21: [K2tog] 6 times (6 sts).

Break yarn and draw tightly through the stitches with a tapestry needle.

Lay the piece flat and, without stuffing it, seam the open cast-on edges using mattress stitch.

FINISHING

With C, stitch eyes on top of the body, just behind the cuff, with 2 stitches that cross for each eye.

All the following appendages should be attached to the body by their cast-on edges, using mattress stitch.

Attach legs to either end of the bottom edge of the body, and arms to either end of the bottom edge of the cuff.

Attach ears to the sides of the body, 6 stitches back from the mouth.

Flatten the tongue, lining up the two holes to form one buttonhole. Attach the tongue to the middle top edge of the mouth.

Fold the tongue around the open mouth, and note where the buttonhole sits on the bottom of the body. Attach the button at this place (above).

Weave in loose ends.

TECHNIQUES

Provisional cast-on (page 137), picking up stitches (page 30), backward loop cast-on (page 136), 3-needle bind-off (page 141), mattress stitch (page 23), duplicate stitch (page 32), I-cord (page 138)

YARN

Worsted-weight yarn in 2 colors and black

Samples knit with Cascade 220, 100% wool, 3½ oz (100g), 220 yds (201m), 1 skein each 9076 Mint (A), 8509 Grey (B), 8555 Black (C)

NEEDLES

Set of five 7" (18cm) size 5 US (3.75mm) double-pointed needles

OTHER MATERIALS AND TOOLS

1 set size 12mm safety eyes, 2 sets size 9mm safety eyes, stuffing

FINISHED SIZE

Approx 5½" (14cm) wide and 3½" (9cm) tall (not including toast)

TOASTER GHOST

· · · · · · · · · · · · · · · · · ·

Formerly a cooperative household appliance, this toaster turned rogue after dying from one too many frozen waffles crammed into his slots. Now he takes his supernatural revenge by burning every piece of bread in sight.

· · · · · · · · · · · · · · ● · · · · · · · · · · · ·

· · · · · · **F A C T S** · · · · · ·

LIKES: The cute blender across the counter

HATES: Toaster ovens (a far inferior appliance)

EATS: Crumbs, the darker the better

HAUNTS: Old kitchens and yard sales

TOASTER

BASE

Using a provisional cast-on with waste yarn and a crochet hook, cast on 20 stitches of A onto one needle to work straight.

Beginning with a purl row, work 40 rows in stockinette stitch.

SIDES

Instead of turning for the next purl row, rotate the piece 90 degrees clockwise, and pick up and knit 30 stitches along the side of the piece with a second needle. Undo and remove the waste yarn and place those 20 stitches on a third needle, and knit. With a fourth needle, pick up and knit 30 stitches along the remaining side (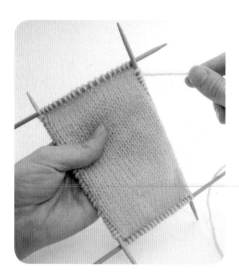).

A Once the base is complete, pick up stitches on the other three sides of the piece and begin knitting in the round.

You will continue to knit these 100 stitches in a round, using a fifth needle.

RND 1: First needle: K20; second needle: k30; third needle: k20; fourth needle: k30.

RNDS 2–15: Knit.

RND 16: [K20, k2tog, k to last 2 stitches on the needle, k2tog] twice (96 sts).

RNDS 17 AND 18: Knit.

RND 19: [K2tog, k to last 2 stitches on the same needle, k2tog] 4 times (88 sts).

RNDS 20 AND 21: Knit.

RND 22: [K18, k2tog, k to last 2 stitches on the same needle, k2tog] twice (84 sts).

RND 23: Knit.

RND 24: Work same as Rnd 19 (76 sts).

RND 25: Knit.

Bind off all stitches.

SLOTS

With B, cast on 24 stitches onto one needle to work straight.

Beginning with a purl row, work 5 rows in stockinette stitch.

ROW 6: K4, BO 16 (begin binding off with the 5th and 6th sts), k3 (8 sts).

ROW 7: P4, cast on 16 stitches using the backward loop method, p4 (24 sts).

ROWS 8–13: Work 6 rows in stockinette stitch as established.

ROW 14: K4, BO 16, k3 (8 sts).

ROW 15: P4, cast on 16 using the backward loop method, p4 (24 sts).

ROWS 16–20: Work 5 rows in stockinette stitch as established.

Bind off all stitches purlwise.

POCKETS

(MAKE 2, ONE FOR EACH HOLE IN THE SLOTS PIECE)

Hold the slots piece with the knit side facing you, and using B, pick up and knit 32 stitches around one hole left by the bind-off/cast-on stitches that you made midway through the piece—pick up the 16 bound-off stitches and the 16 cast-on stitches (**B**).

Distribute stitches onto 3 needles, and join to work in a round.

Knit 16 rounds.

Divide stitches onto 2 needles, and bind off using a 3-needle bind-off.

Turn the pocket inside out, so that the knit stitches form the inside of the slot. With a tapestry needle, close up the small holes left in the piece with 1 or 2 small stitches for each.

LEVER

With B, cast on 6 stitches onto 3 DPNs and join to work in a round.

RND 1: [Kfb] 6 times (12 sts).

RND 2: Kfb, k4, [kfb] twice, k4, kfb (16 sts).

RNDS 3–8: Knit (6 rnds).

RND 9: K2tog, k4, [k2tog] twice, k4, k2tog (12 sts).

Stuff piece.

RND 10: [K2tog] 6 times (6 sts).

Break yarn and draw tightly through the stitches with a tapestry needle.

DIAL

With B, cast on 18 stitches onto 3 DPNs and join to work in a round.

RNDS 1–3: Knit.

RND 4: [K2tog, k1] 6 times (12 sts).

RND 5: [K2tog] 6 times (6 sts).

Break yarn and draw tightly through the stitches with a tapestry needle.

FINISHING TOASTER

Attach eyes midway down on one of the long sides of the toaster, spaced about 9 stitches apart. With C, embroider eyebrows with one long, diagonal stitch for each.

Place the slot piece on top of the toaster piece, with the outer rectangle of the slot piece aligning with the bound-off edge of the toaster. Beginning in one corner, seam together using mattress stitch (**C**).

Stuff the toaster before you finish seaming, making sure to stuff fully, including the space between the slots, without overstuffing.

With C, use duplicate stitch to make a row of 16 vertical stitches on the side of the toaster.

Attach the side of the lever to the area with duplicate stitch using mattress stitch.

B To begin making a pocket in a slot, pick up and knit the cast-on and bound-off stitches that you left in the piece.

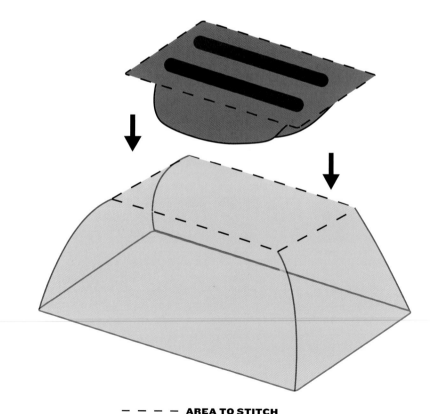

– – – – AREA TO STITCH

C Align the sides of the slot piece with the bound-off edge of the toaster and seam in place using mattress stitch.

D After making a row of duplicate stitch, attach the lever and dial to the side of the toaster. The stitches for the cord should be picked up from the back side.

Attach the cast-on edge of the dial to the side of the toaster using mattress stitch, stuffing the piece before closing up the seam (**D**).

CORD

With C, pick up and knit 4 stitches at the back of the toaster, toward the bottom, picking up between knitted stitches so that they are close together.

Work in I-cord until the cord is about 4" long, then continue to knit in a round as follows.

RND 1: [Kfb] 4 times, and distribute 8 stitches onto 3 DPNs.

RND 2: [Kfb] 8 times (16 sts).

RNDS 3–5: Knit.

Stuff the piece.

RND 6: [K2tog] 8 times (8 sts).

Break yarn and draw through the stitches.

For prongs, with B, cast on 2 stitches onto one needle, and knit an I-cord 1½" (3.8cm) long. Thread through the end of the plug, leaving an equal amount of each end of the I-cord sticking out.

Weave in all loose ends.

TOAST (MAKE 2)

With C, cast on 16 stitches onto one needle to work straight.

Beginning with a purl row, work 13 rows in stockinette stitch.

ROW 14: K1, [kfb] 3 times, k8, [kfb] 3 times, k1 (22 sts).

ROWS 15–17: Work 3 rows in stockinette stitch as established.

ROW 18: K1, [k2tog] twice, k12, [k2tog] twice, k1 (18 sts).

ROW 19: Purl.

ROW 20: K1, [k2tog] twice, k8, [k2tog] twice, k1 (14 sts).

ROW 21: Purl.

ROW 22: K1, [kfb] twice, k8, [kfb] twice, k1 (18 sts).

ROW 23: Purl.

ROW 24: K1, [kfb] twice, k12, [kfb] twice, k1 (22 sts).

ROWS 25–27: Work 3 rows in stockinette stitch as established.

ROW 28: K1, [k2tog] 3 times, k8, [k2tog] 3 times, k1 (16 st).

ROWS 29–41: Work 13 rows in stockinette stitch as established.

Bind off all stitches (**E**).

FINISHING TOAST

Fold the toast piece in half horizontally, with the knit stitches on the outside.

Attach the eyes midway down one side, spaced 5 stitches apart.

Sew all edges together using mattress stitch, and stuff lightly before closing up.

Weave in loose ends.

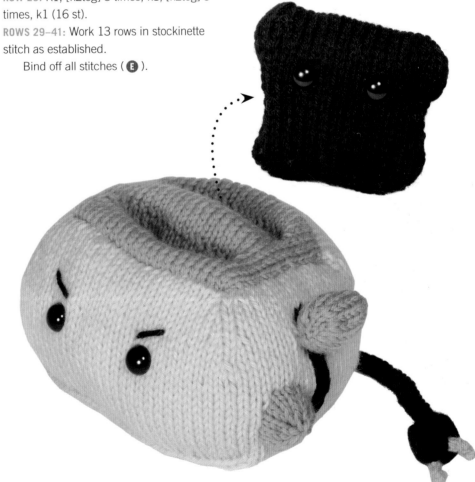

E Before being folded in half and seamed, the toast piece widens twice in the middle.

MIX 'N' MATCH MONSTERS

....

Get your maniacal laugh ready—it's time to play Mad Scientist Knitter!
(Spooky lab equipment is not required, but it sure looks cool.)

....

Create a
CUSTOM
Super-Scary Mochi

This section serves up a full menu of dismembered bodies and disembodied bits so you can create a monster mochi that's your own unique creation. Mwuhahaha!

Bodies

Thin or thick, curvy or sharp, your monster's bod is the starting point for all the madness.

ROUND

SAMPLE YARN: Cascade 220 in 9542 Blaze
Cast on 4 stitches onto one needle.
RND 1 (WORK AS AN I-CORD): [Kfb] 4 times (8 sts).

Distribute stitches onto 3 DPNs to continue to work in a round.
RND 2: [Kfb] 8 times (16 sts).
RND 3 AND ALL ODD-NUMBERED RNDS THROUGH RND 13: Knit.

RND 4: [Kfb, k1] 8 times (24 sts).
RND 6: [Kfb, k2] 8 times (32 sts).
RND 8: [Kfb, k3] 8 times (40 sts).
RND 10: [Kfb, k4] 8 times (48 sts).
RND 12: [Kfb, k5] 8 times (56 sts).
RND 14: [Kfb, k6] 8 times (64 sts).
RNDS 15–17: Knit.
RND 18: [Kfb, k7] 8 times (72 sts).
RNDS 19–21: Knit.
RND 22: [Kfb, k8] 8 times (80 sts).
RNDS 23–25: Knit.
RND 26: [Kfb, k9] 8 times (88 sts).
RNDS 27–38: Knit 12 rnds.
RND 39: [K2tog, k9] 8 times (80 sts).
RNDS 40–42: Knit.

DO IT YOURSELF

The samples shown are made with worsted-weight wool yarn, but don't be afraid to mix different scrap yarns, add bizarre buttons for eyes, or experiment with other strange embellishments.

Since you will make your own unique monster, placement of eyes and limbs is entirely up to you, and no guidelines are given.

I recommend using mattress stitch to attach limbs, but you can also use whipstitch for a cobbled-together effect. Add other fun details like scars and gashes with some simple embroidery. Be creative and make your monster as scary or silly as you like!

Make your own monster
FACTS

NAME: _____

LIKES: _____

_____

HATES: _____

_____

EATS: _____

_____

HAUNTS: _____

_____

RND 43: [K2tog, k8] 8 times (72 sts).

RNDS 44–46: Knit.

RND 47: [K2tog, k7] 8 times (64 sts).

RNDS 48–50: Knit.

RND 51: [K2tog, k6] 8 times (56 sts).

RND 52 AND ALL EVEN-NUMBERED RNDS THROUGH RND 60: Knit.

RND 53: [K2tog, k5] 8 times (48 sts).

RND 55: [K2tog, k4] 8 times (40 sts).

RND 57: [K2tog, k3] 8 times (32 sts).

RND 59: [K2tog, k2] 8 times (24 sts).

Stuff the piece and attach eyes.

RND 61: [K2tog, k1] 8 times (16 sts).

RND 62: [K2tog] 8 times.

Break yarn and draw tightly through the stitches with a tapestry needle.

Weave in loose ends.

TALL

SAMPLE YARN: Cascade 220 in 7828 Neon Yellow

Cast on 4 stitches onto one needle.

RND 1 (WORK AS AN I-CORD): [Kfb] 4 times (8 sts).

Distribute stitches onto 3 DPNs to continue to work in a round.

RND 2: [Kfb] 8 times (16 sts).

RND 3 AND ALL ODD-NUMBERED RNDS THROUGH RND 9: Knit.

RND 4: [Kfb, k1] 8 times (24 sts).

RND 6: [Kfb, k2] 8 times (32 sts).

RND 8: [Kfb, k3] 8 times (40 sts).

RND 10: [Kfb, k4] 8 times (48 sts).

RNDS 11–70: Knit 60 rounds.

RND 71: [K2tog, k6] 6 times (42 sts).

RND 72 AND ALL EVEN-NUMBERED RNDS THROUGH RND 80: Knit.

RND 73: [K2tog, k5] 6 times (36 sts).

RND 75: [K2tog, k4] 6 times (30 sts).

RND 77: [K2tog, k3] 6 times (24 sts).

Stuff the piece and attach eyes.

RND 79: [K2tog, k2] 6 times (18 sts).

RND 81: [K2tog] 9 times (9 sts).

Break yarn and draw tightly through the stitches with a tapestry needle.

Weave in loose ends.

SQUAT

SAMPLE YARN: Cascade 220 in 8907 Caribbean

BOTTOM SECTION

Cast on 4 stitches onto one needle.

RND 1 (WORK AS I-CORD): [Kfb] 4 times (8 sts).

Distribute stitches onto 3 DPNs to continue to work in a round.

RND 2: [Kfb] 8 times (16 sts).

RND 3: Knit.

RND 4: [Kfb, k1] 8 times (24 sts).

RND 5: Knit.

RND 6: [Kfb, k2] 8 times (32 sts).

Continue to increase 8 stitches every other round until there are 112 stitches on your needles. (In each increase round, the number of stitches to be knitted following the kfb will increase by one.) If it's more comfortable for you, as the number of stitches increases, you can add a fourth DPN to hold the stitches, and knit with a fifth DPN.

Knit 9 rounds.

TOP SECTION

RND 1: [K2tog, k12] 8 times (104 sts).

RND 2: Knit.

RND 3: [K2tog, k11] 8 times (96 sts).

RND 4: Knit.

RND 5: [K2tog, k10] 8 times (88 sts).

Continue to decrease 8 stitches every other round until there are 24 stitches on your needles.

Stuff the piece, pressing it flat as you do to avoid overstuffing. Attach eyes.

FINAL DECREASE

RND 1: Knit.

RND 2: [K2tog, k1] 8 times (16 sts).

RND 3: [K2tog] 8 times (8 sts).

Break yarn, leaving a long tail, and draw tightly through the stitches with a tapestry needle. When you weave in the tail, hold the piece flat and loosely weave the tail through the body several times to retain the flat shape (opposite, top).

Weave in loose ends.

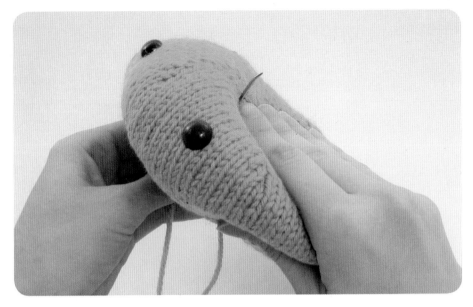

When weaving in the tail end of the Squat Body, hold the body flat to help it keep its shape.

RND 43: [K2tog, k9] 8 times (80 sts)

RNDS 44–47: Knit.

RND 48: [Kfb, k9] 8 times (88 sts).

RNDS 49–51: Knit.

RND 52: [Kfb, k10] twice, then place the next 44 stitches on a holder. Pulling yarn tightly behind the held stitches, finish the round with [kfb, k10] twice. (See Separating Pieces, page 29.)

Redistribute the 48 working stitches onto 3 DPNs to continue to work in a round.

RNDS 53–68: Knit 16 rounds.

RND 69: [K2tog, k6] 6 times (42 sts).

RND 70 AND ALL EVEN-NUMBERED RNDS THROUGH RND 78: Knit.

RND 71: [K2tog, k5] 6 times (36 sts).

RND 73: [K2tog, k4] 6 times (30 sts).

RND 75: [K2tog, k3] 6 times (24 sts).

TWO-HEADED

SAMPLE YARN: Cascade 220 in 9469 Hot Pink

Cast on 4 stitches onto one needle.

RND 1 (WORK AS AN I-CORD): [Kfb] 4 times (8 sts).

Distribute stitches onto 3 DPNs to continue to work in a round.

RND 2: [Kfb] 8 times (16 sts).

RND 3 AND ALL ODD-NUMBERED RNDS THROUGH RND 13: Knit.

RND 4: [Kfb, k1] 8 times (24 sts).

RND 6: [Kfb, k2] 8 times (32 sts).

RND 8: [Kfb, k3] 8 times (40 sts).

RND 10: [Kfb, k4] 8 times (48 sts).

RND 12: [Kfb, k5] 8 times (56 sts).

RND 14: [Kfb, k6] 8 times (64 sts).

RNDS 15–17: Knit.

RND 18: [Kfb, k7] 8 times (72 sts).

RNDS 19–21: Knit.

RND 22: [Kfb, k8] 8 times (80 sts).

RNDS 23–25: Knit.

RND 26: [Kfb, k9] 8 times (88 sts).

RNDS 27–29: Knit.

RND 30: [Kfb, k10] 8 times (96 sts).

RNDS 31–38: Knit 8 rnds.

RND 39: [K2tog, k10] 8 times (88 sts).

RNDS 40–42: Knit.

Leaving the body unstuffed, attach eyes to this head.

RND 77: [K2tog, k2] 6 times (18 sts).

RND 79: [K2tog] 9 times (9 sts).

Break yarn and draw tightly through the stitches with a tapestry needle.

Place the 44 held stitches onto 3 DPNs, and reattach the yarn to the last stitch (the rightmost stitch on purl side). Join to work in a round.

RND 80: [Kfb, k10] 4 times (48 sts).

RNDS 81–96: Knit 16 rounds.

RND 97: [K2tog, k6] 6 times (42 sts).

RND 98 AND ALL EVEN-NUMBERED RNDS THROUGH RND 106: Knit.

RND 99: [K2tog, k5] 6 times (36 sts).

RND 101: [K2tog, k4] 6 times (30 sts).

RND 103: [K2tog, k3] 6 times (24 sts).

Stuff the entire body, making sure to fill out the first head, and attach eyes to this head.

RND 105: [K2tog, k2] 6 times (18 sts).

RND 107: [K2tog] 9 times (9 sts).

Break yarn and draw tightly through the stitches with a tapestry needle.

Close the gap between the heads with a couple of small stitches.

CUBE

SAMPLE YARN: Cascade 220 in 7814 Chartreuse

BASE

Using a crochet hook and waste yarn, provisionally cast on 26 stitches.

Beginning with a purl row, work 32 rows in stockinette stitch.

SIDES

Instead of turning for the next purl row, rotate the piece 90 degrees clockwise, and pick up and knit 26 stitches along the side of the piece with a second DPN. Undo and remove the waste yarn, place those 26 stitches on a third DPN, and knit. With a fourth DPN, pick up and knit 26 stitches along the remaining side. You will have 104 stitches on your needles (A).

Using a fifth DPN to knit, knit 24 rounds.

NEXT RND: K26, BO to end, binding off the last stitch with the first stitch in the next round.

You will have one stitch on the needle in your right hand, and 25 on the needle in your left. Continue to knit to the end of the row.

TOP

Turn the piece and, beginning with a purl row, work 31 rows in stockinette stitch.

BO all stitches.

Fold the top down so that it aligns with the previous bound-off stitches, and begin seaming the top to the sides using mattress stitch (B).

Before you finish seaming, attach eyes and stuff the piece fully, making sure to fill out all the corners.

A Once the base is complete, pick up stitches on the other three sides of the piece and begin knitting in the round.

B After completing the flap, fold the flap down, and seam the edges to the earlier bound-off stitches using mattress stitch.

Facial Features

Somebody is due for a freaky facial! What kind of mug will you give your beastie baby?

FANG

SAMPLE YARN: Cascade 220 in 9076 Mint (A) and 8555 Black (B)

With A, cast on 3 stitches onto one needle.

Knit 4 rows as an I-cord, then break yarn and draw tightly through the stitches with a tapestry needle.

With the end still threaded on the tapestry needle, insert the needle into the body and pull the I-cord into the body just enough to hide the end of the I-cord. With the tail you left at cast-on, tack the tip of the fang down.

With B, embroider a straight line with backstitch along the top of the fang(s).

TONGUE

SAMPLE YARN: Cascade 220 in 9478 Cotton Candy (A) and 8555 Black (B)

With A, cast on 4 stitches onto one needle to work straight.

Beginning with a purl row, work 9 rows in stockinette stitch.

NEXT ROW: [K2tog] twice (2 sts).

Break yarn, leaving a tail, and draw tightly through the stitches with a tapestry needle.

Place the purl side against body, and attach the cast-on edge to the body using mattress stitch. With the tail end you left, tack down the tip of the tongue.

With B, embroider a straight line with backstitch along the top of the tongue.

MUSTACHE

SAMPLE YARN: Cascade 220 in 9471 Amber

Cast on 3 stitches onto one needle. You will work the first 5 rounds as an I-cord.

RND 1: Knit.

RND 2: Kfb, k2 (4 sts).

RNDS 3 AND 4: Knit.

RND 5: Kfb, k2, kfb (6 sts).

Distribute the stitches onto 3 DPNs to continue to work in a round.

RNDS 6 AND 7: Knit.

RND 8: Kfb, k4, kfb (8 sts).

RNDS 9 AND 10: Knit.

Insert a small amount of stuffing into the piece.

Divide the stitches onto 2 DPNs for the next 2 rounds.

RND 11: [K2tog] 4 times (4 sts).

RND 12: [Kfb] 4 times (8 sts).

Distribute the stitches onto 3 DPNs.

RNDS 13 AND 14: Knit 2 rounds.

Insert another small amount of stuffing into the piece.

RND 15: K2tog, k4, k2tog (6 sts).

RNDS 16 AND 17: Knit.

RND 18: K2tog, k2, k2tog (4 sts).

Place the stitches onto one needle to work as an I-cord.

RNDS 19 AND 20: Knit.

RND 21: K2tog, k2 (3 sts).

RND 22: Knit.

Break yarn and draw tightly through the stitches with a tapestry needle.

Curl the tips of the piece up, and attach to the body with a few stitches at the back of the piece.

CLOWN NOSE

SAMPLE YARN: Cascade 220 in 8414 Bright Red

Cast on 8 stitches onto 3 DPNs and join in a round.

RND 1: Knit.

RND 2: [Kfb] 8 times (16 sts).

RND 3: [Kfb, k1] 8 times (24 sts).

RNDS 4–7: Knit.

RND 8: [K2tog, k2] 6 times (18 sts).

RND 9: Knit.

Stuff the piece.

RND 10: [K2tog, k1] 6 times (12 sts).

RND 11: [K2tog] 6 times (6 sts).

Break yarn and draw tightly through the stitches with a tapestry needle.

BEAK

SAMPLE YARN: Cascade 220 in 7828 Neon Yellow

Cast on 12 stitches onto 3 DPNs and join in a round.

RND 1: Knit.

RND 2: [Kfb, k2] 4 times (16 sts).

RND 3: Kfb, k3, place next 8 stitches on a safety pin or a spare needle. Pulling yarn tightly behind the held stitches, finish off the round with k3, kfb. (See Separating Pieces, page 29.)

Redistribute the 10 working stitches onto 3 DPNs to continue to work in a round.

RNDS 4–8: Knit 5 rounds.

RND 9: [K2tog] 5 times (5 sts).

Break yarn and draw tightly through the stitches with a tapestry needle.

Reattach the yarn to the last stitch on the spare needle (the rightmost stitch on the purl side). Distribute 8 stitches onto 3 DPNs, and join to work in a round.

RND 10: K3, [kfb] twice, k3 (10 sts).

RNDS 11–13: Knit.

RND 14: [K2tog] 5 times (5 sts).

Break yarn and draw tightly through the stitches with a tapestry needle.

Close the gap between the top and bottom of the beak with a couple of small stitches.

Stuff the piece, and attach to the body with the longer side on top.

Headgear

Crown your creature with something strange and stylish.

STRIPY HORN

SAMPLE YARN: Cascade 220 in 8505 White (A) and 8907 Caribbean (B)

With A, cast on 12 stitches onto 3 DPNs and join in a round.

RND 1: Knit.

Switch to B.

RNDS 2 AND 3: Knit.

Switch to A.

RNDS 4 AND 5: Knit.

Switch to B.

RNDS 6 AND 7: Knit.

Switch to A.

RND 8: K2tog, k to last 2 sts, k2tog (10 sts).

RND 9: Knit.

Switch to B.

RND 10: K2tog, k to last 2 sts, k2tog (8 sts).

RND 11: Knit.

Switch to A.

RND 12: K2tog, k to last 2 sts, k2tog (6 sts).

RND 13: Knit.

Break yarn and draw tightly through the stitches.

Stuff the piece.

ANTENNA

SAMPLE YARN: Cascade 220 in 9076 Mint (A) and 7808 Purple Hyacinth (B)

With A, cast on 6 stitches onto 3 DPNs and join in a round.

RNDS 1–11: Knit.

Switch to B.

RND 12: Knit.

RND 13: [Kfb] 6 times (12 sts).

RND 14: [Kfb, k2] 4 times (16 sts).

RNDS 15–18: Knit.

Stuff the wider section of the piece, leaving the thinner section unstuffed.

RND 19: [K2tog] 8 times (8 sts).

Break yarn and draw tightly through the stitches with a tapestry needle.

For poseable antenna, you can use a pipe cleaner. Cut the pipe cleaner to twice the length of the thinner section of the piece, fold it in half, and twist it tightly. Insert the folded end of the pipe cleaner into the piece from the cast-on opening.

SPIKE

SAMPLE YARN: Cascade 220 in 9542 Blaze

Cast on 16 stitches onto 3 DPNs and join to work in a round.

RNDS 1–4: Knit.

RND 5: K2tog, k4, [k2tog] twice, k4, k2tog (12 sts).

RNDS 6 AND 7: Knit.

RND 8: K2tog, k2, [k2tog] twice, k2, k2tog (8 sts).

RND 9: Knit.

RND 10: [K2tog] 4 times (4 sts).

Break yarn and draw tightly through the stitches with a tapestry needle.

Pinch the piece flat and stuff lightly.

BOLT

SAMPLE YARN: Cascade 220 in 8509 Grey (A) and 8555 Black (B)

With A, cast on 8 stitches onto 3 DPNs and join to work in a round.

RNDS 1–8: Knit.

RND 9: [Kfb] 8 times (16 sts).

RND 10: Knit.

RND 11: [Kfb, k1] 8 times (24 sts).

RNDS 12 AND 13: Knit.

RND 14: [K2tog, k1] 8 times (16 sts).

Stuff the piece.

RND 15: [K2tog] 8 times (8 sts).

Break yarn and draw tightly through the stitches with a tapestry needle.

Pinch the larger section flat when closing up and weaving in the tail. With B, embroider one straight stitch onto the top.

WOOLY EAR

SAMPLE YARN: Cascade 220 in 7814 Chartreuse (A) and 9471 Amber (B)

NOTE: You will also need a crochet hook.

With A, cast on 16 stitches onto 3 DPNs and join to work in a round.

RND 1: Knit.

RND 2: K5, p6, k5.

RND 3: K5, p2tog, p2, p2tog, k5 (14 sts).

RNDS 4 AND 5: K5, p4, k5.

RND 6: K5, [p2tog] twice, k5 (12 sts).

RNDS 7 AND 8: K5, p2, k5.

RND 9: K4, [k2tog] twice, k4 (10 sts).

RND 10: [K2tog] 5 times (5 sts).

Break yarn and draw tightly through the stitches with a tapestry needle.

For hair, cut 3 strands of B about 3" (7.5cm) in length. Insert a crochet hook under a stitch on the purl section of the ear, fold one strand in half, and use the crochet hook to pull the yarn through. Tuck the loose ends of the yarn through the loop that you've pulled through, and pull tightly. (See Using a Crochet Hook to Attach Hair, page 33.)

Use the tip of a pair of sharp scissors to separate the individual strands of hair for a shaggy look. Trim to desired length.

Stuff the piece.

GO NUTS!

Using the pieces shown as examples, it's easy to create your own original weird body parts. Experimenting with shapes and colors can lead to all kinds of new monster magic.

SYMMETRY IS OVERRATED

The sample monsters shown have matching parts, but don't be afraid to mix it up with bizarro appendage combinations.

Arms and Legs

Will your mochi grab, pinch, hug, or high-five? Give 'em as many appendages as you can handle!

PAW

SAMPLE YARN: Cascade 220 in 9471 Amber (A) and 7828 Neon Yellow (B)

With A, cast on 6 stitches onto 3 DPNs and join in a round.

RND 1: [Kfb] 6 times (12 sts).

RNDS 2 AND 3: Knit.

RND 4: Kfb, k4, [kfb] twice, k4, kfb (16 sts).

RNDS 5 AND 6: Knit.

RND 7: Kfb, k6, [kfb] twice, k6, kfb (20 sts).

RND 8: Knit.

RND 9: Kfb, k8, [kfb] twice, k8, kfb (24 sts).

RNDS 10–13: Knit.

RND 14: [K2tog, k1] 8 times (16 sts).

RND 15: [K2tog, yo] 4 times, k8 (16 sts).

Stuff the piece, then divide the stitches onto 2 needles and bind off using Kitchener stitch.

CLAWS

With B, cast on 4 stitches onto one needle.

Knit 9 rows of I-cord.

Break yarn and draw tightly through the stitches with a tapestry needle, then thread the I-cord through the middle 2 yarn-over holes on the paw.

Knit another I-cord with 13 rows, and thread this longer piece through the first and last yarn-over holes in the paw.

Weave in loose ends.

TENTACLE

SAMPLE YARN: Cascade 220 in 9478 Cotton Candy (A) and 7808 Purple Hyacinth (B)

With A, cast on 16 stitches onto 3 DPNs and join in a round.

RND 1: Knit.

RND 2 AND ALL EVEN-NUMBERED RNDS THROUGH RND 28: Knit.

RND 3: Knit.

RND 5: Kfb, k to last st, kfb (18 sts).

RND 7: Kfb, k6, [k2tog] twice, k6, kfb (18 sts).

RND 9: Kfb, k to last st, kfb (20 sts).

RND 11: Kfb, k7, [k2tog] twice, k7, kfb (20 sts).

RND 13: Work same as Rnd 11.

RND 15: Work same as Rnd 11.

RND 17: K8, [k2tog] twice, k8 (18 sts).

RND 19: Kfb, k6, [k2tog] twice, k6, kfb (18 sts).

RND 21: Kfb, k4, [k2tog] 4 times, k4, kfb (16 sts).

RND 23: Kfb, k5, [k2tog] twice, k5, kfb (16 sts).

RND 25: Kfb, k3, [k2tog] 4 times, k3, kfb (14 sts).

RND 27: Kfb, k2, [k2tog] 4 times, k2, kfb (12 sts).

RND 29: [K2tog] 6 times (6 sts).

Break yarn and draw tightly through the stitches with a tapestry needle.

Stuff the piece.

With B, embroider 2 rows of suckers, with 2 horizontal stitches for each, on one side of the piece.

CLAW

SAMPLE YARN: Cascade 220 in 7828 Neon Yellow (A) and 9469 Hot Pink (B)

With A, cast on 10 stitches onto 3 DPNs and join in a round.

RNDS 1–3: Knit.

RND 4: Purl.

Repeat the above 4 rounds 5 times total, then knit 2 more rounds. Stuff the piece before continuing.

SHAPE CLAW

Switch to B.

RND 1: Knit.

RND 2: [Kfb] 10 times (20 sts).

RNDS 3 AND 4: Knit.

RND 5: Kfb, k4, then place the next 10 stitches on a spare needle to work later. Pulling yarn tightly behind the held stitches, finish off the round with k4, kfb. (See Separating Pieces, page 29.)

Redistribute the 12 working stitches onto 3 DPNs to continue to work in a round.

RNDS 6–9: Knit.

RND 10: [K2tog] twice, k4, [k2tog] twice (8 sts).

RND 11: Knit.

Stuff the piece.

RND 12: [K2tog] 4 times (4 sts).

Break yarn and draw tightly through the stitches.

Reattach the yarn to the last stitch on the spare needle (the rightmost stitch on the purl side). Distribute 10 stitches onto 3 DPNs, and join to work in a round.

RND 13: K4, [kfb] twice, k4 (12 sts).

RNDS 14–17: Knit.

RND 18: K2, [k2tog] 4 times, k2 (8 sts).

RND 19: Knit.

Stuff the piece.

RND 20: [K2tog] 4 times (4 sts).

Break yarn and draw tightly through the stitches.

Close the gap between the two sides of the claw with a couple of small stitches.

BAT WING

SAMPLE YARN: Cascade 220 in 8555 Black
Cast on 8 stitches onto one needle to work straight.

ROW 1 AND ALL ODD-NUMBERED ROWS THROUGH ROW13: Purl.

ROW 2: K1, kfb, k to last 2 sts, kfb, k1 (10 sts).

ROW 4: Work same as Row 2 (12 sts).

ROW 6: Knit.

ROW 8: Work same as Row 2 (14 sts).

ROW 10: Knit.

ROW 12: Work same as Row 2 (16 sts).

ROW 14: K3, BO 4 (begin binding off with 4th and 5th sts), k1, BO 4, k2 (8 sts).

After working Row 14, you will have a group of 3 stitches on each end of the piece, and a set of 2 stitches in the middle.

Purl 3 stitches, then turn, and knit 3 stitches.

Break yarn, leaving a tail of about 16" (40.5cm). Thread the tail of yarn on a tapestry needle, and slip through the 3 stitches you just worked, from right to left, then slip the stitches off the needle and pull tightly.

Weave the tail through the back (purl) side of the piece, and rejoin with the next 2 stitches in the purl row.

Purl 2 stitches, then turn, and knit 2 stitches. Thread the tail through these stitches right to left and slip off the needle.

Weave the tail through the back of the piece, and rejoin with the last 3 stitches. Repeat the same technique used with the previous stitches to finish off.

Block the piece by dampening it and laying it flat to dry, pinning out the 3 wing tips to make them more prominent.

VINE

SAMPLE YARN: Cascade 220 in 7814 Chartreuse

Cast on 9 stitches onto 3 DPNs and join in a round.

RNDS 1–12: Knit, stuffing the piece as you go.

RND 13: [K2tog, k1] 3 times (6 sts).

RNDS 14–25: Knit 12 rounds, stuffing the piece as you go.

RND 26: [K2tog] 3 times (3 sts).

Place stitches onto one needle to work as an I-cord, and knit 9 rounds.

Break yarn, leaving a long tail, and draw tightly through the stitches with a tapestry needle. Weave the tail in and out

vertically along the edge of the piece and pull, making the piece curl in.

LEAF (MAKE 3, OR AS MANY OR FEW AS YOU LIKE)

Pick up and knit 2 stitches from the main piece.

ROW 1: Knit one row of I-cord.

ROW 2 (WORK AS AN I-CORD): [Kfb] twice (4 sts).

Turn to work straight.

ROW 3: Purl.

ROW 4: Knit.

ROW 5: [P2tog] twice (2 sts).

Break yarn and draw tightly through the stitches with a tapestry needle.

TENDRIL

Cast on 30 stitches onto one needle to work straight.

K2tog, [k2tog, pass rightmost stitch over] repeat to the end, binding off as you go until the last stitch is bound off.

Attach the tendril to the center of the main piece.

Tails

Your creature should be just as scary going as it is coming, so don't forget to address the rear.

WILD TAIL

SAMPLE YARN: Cascade 220 in 7828 Neon Yellow (A) and 8907 Caribbean (B)

With A, cast on 8 stitches onto 3 DPNs and join to work in a round.

RNDS 1–40: Knit, stuffing the piece as you go.

Switch to B.

RND 41: Knit.

RND 42: [Kfb] 8 times (16 sts).

RND 43: [K1, p1] to end.

RND 44: [Kfb, k3] 4 times (20 sts).

RNDS 45–48: [K1, p2, k1, p1] 4 times.

RND 49: [K2tog, p1, k1, p1] 4 times (16 sts).

RND 50: [K1, p1] to end.

RND 51: [K2tog, k1, p1] 4 times (12 sts).

RND 52: [K2, p1] to end.

Stuff the end of the piece.

RND 53: [K2tog, p1] 4 times (8 sts).

RND 54: [K2tog] 4 times (4 sts).

Break yarn and draw tightly through the stitches with a tapestry needle.

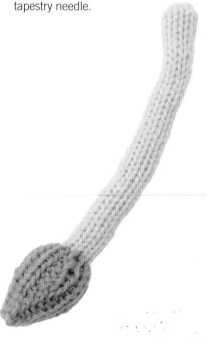

SPIKY TAIL

SAMPLE YARN: Cascade 220 in 9542 Blaze (A) and 7828 Neon Yellow (B)

With A, cast on 9 stitches onto 3 DPNs and join to work in a round.

Knit 9 rounds.

RND 10: [Kfb, k2] 3 times (12 sts).

RNDS 11 AND 12: Knit.

RND 13: [Kfb, k3] 3 times (15 sts).

RNDS 14 AND 15: Knit.

RND 16: [Kfb, k4] 3 times (18 sts).

RNDS 17 AND 18: Knit.

RND 19: [Kfb, k5] 3 times (21 sts).

RNDS 20 AND 21: Knit.

RND 22: [Kfb, k6] 3 times (24 sts).

RND 23: K5, k2tog, yo, k10, k2tog, yo, k5 (24 sts).

RNDS 24–28: Knit 5 rounds.

RND 29: K5, k2tog, yo, k10, k2tog, yo, k5 (24 sts).

RND 30: Knit.

RND 31: [K2tog, k2] 6 times (18 sts).

RND 32: Knit.

Stuff the piece.

RND 33: [K2tog, k1] 6 times (12 sts).

RND 34: [K2tog] 6 times (6 sts).

Break yarn and draw tightly through the stitches with a tapestry needle.

SPIKES (MAKE 2)

With B, cast on 3 stitches onto one needle.

Knit 18 rows of I-cord, then break yarn and draw tightly through the stitches with a tapestry needle. Thread each I-cord through one set of horizontal yarn-over holes.

Weave in loose ends.

STRIPY TAIL

SAMPLE YARN: Cascade 220 in 9469 Hot Pink (A) and 9076 Mint (B)

With A, cast on 12 stitches onto 3 DPNs and join in a round.

RNDS 1–3: Knit with A.

RNDS 4–6: Knit with B.

Work as established, alternating 3 rounds of A and 3 rounds of B and stuffing as you go, until there are 9 stripes of B.

Switch to A, and knit 3 rounds.

NEXT RND: [K2tog] 6 times (6 sts).

Break yarn and draw tightly through the stitches with a tapestry needle.

$$E + L =$$
$$+$$
$$T$$
$$=$$
$$E \cdot T$$

~ DO THE ~ MONSTER MATH

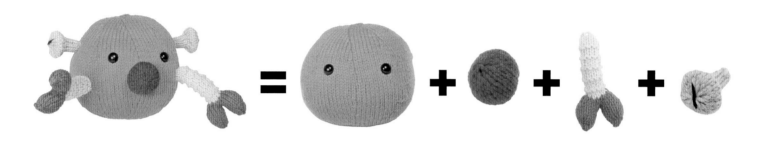

(knit in white)

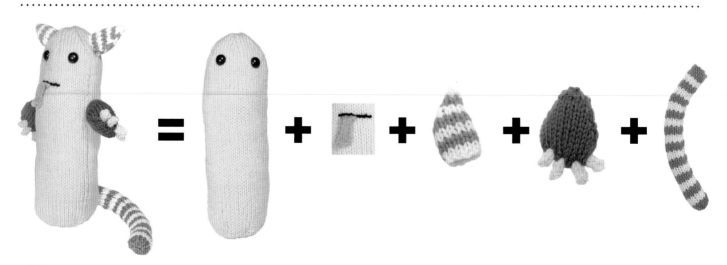

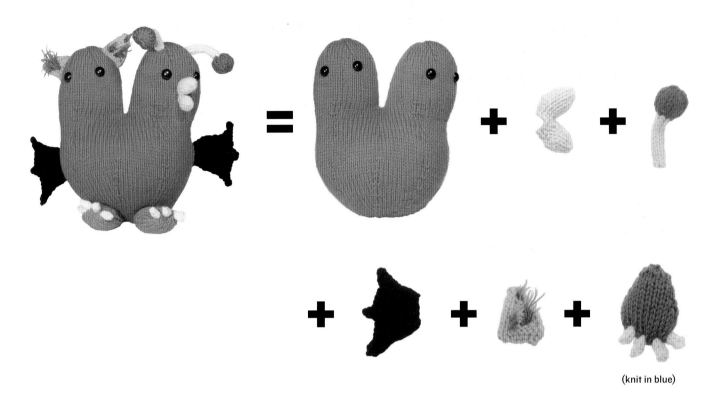

(knit in blue)

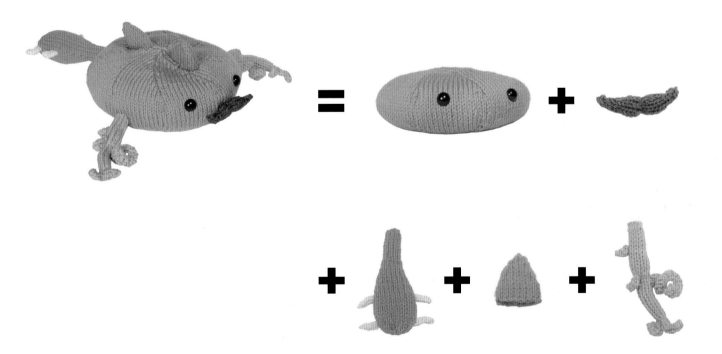

KNITTING ESSENTIALS

BASIC STITCHES

I recommend starting out by learning to knit with two needles, then switching to double-pointed needles (page 18) once you feel comfortable with the basics.

CASTING ON (CO)

The most common way to start a knitting project, unless directions specify otherwise, is with a long-tail cast-on.

Based on the number of stitches to cast on, estimate how much of a tail you will need. For me, with worsted-weight yarn and size 5 US (3.75mm) or size 6 US (4mm) needles, I use about 10" (25.5cm) for every 10 stitches cast on, or 1" (2.5cm) per stitch.

If you are leaving an extra length for seaming, add another 10" (25.5cm) or so to the tail.

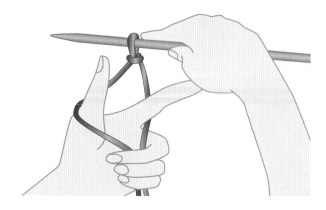

2. Grasp both yarn ends in your left hand, with the yarn attached to the ball around the outside of your thumb and the tail around the outside of your forefinger.

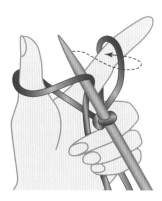

3. With the needle in your right hand, insert the tip of the needle under the outer side of the yarn on your thumb, then dip it over and around the inner side of the yarn on your finger.

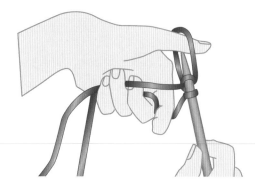

4. Let the yarn slip off your thumb, and pull outward slightly on the stitch you just made to tighten the loop on the needle.

Repeat Steps 2–4, trying to cast on all your stitches with the same tension, until you have the required number of stitches on your needle.

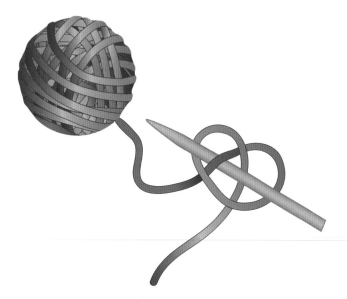

1. Make a slip knot with the yarn, slide the needle through the knot, and tighten. This will become the first stitch in the cast-on.

THE KNIT STITCH (K)

The knit stitch is the most basic stitch.

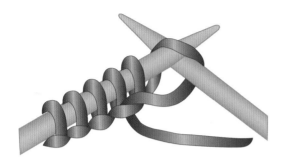

1. Hold the needle with the stitches in your left hand, with the yarn attached to the rightmost stitch. Hold the empty needle in your right hand. (In circular knitting, the attached yarn will be on a different needle—see Using Double-Pointed Needles on page 18.) Insert the tip of the right needle under the front of the first stitch on the left needle.

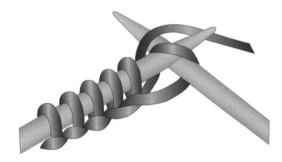

2. Wrap the yarn around the tip of the needle in your right hand, wrapping on top of the needle, from left to right.

3. Pull the right needle back out through the stitch on the left needle, pulling the wrapped yarn out with it.

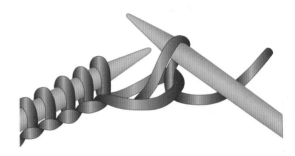

4. Slip the stitch off the left needle. You now have a new stitch on the right needle.

Repeat Steps 1–4 as many times as indicated in the pattern, or until you have transferred all the stitches from the left needle to the right.

When you come to the end of the row:

If you are knitting a flat piece with two needles, switch the right needle to your left hand and flip it around for the next row.

If you are knitting with double-pointed needles, keep the right needle in the same position and move on to knit from the next needle that follows in the round.

THE PURL STITCH (P)

The purl stitch is the reverse of the knit stitch—it happens automatically on the reverse side of knitted stitches. When knitting a flat piece, you flip the piece around to work purl stitches on the reverse side.

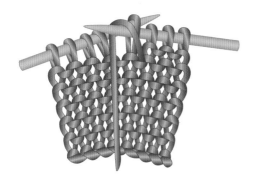

1. Insert the tip of the right needle under the front of the first stitch on the left needle, going in from the right side and coming out in front of the left needle. Wrap the yarn around the top of the needle, from right to left.

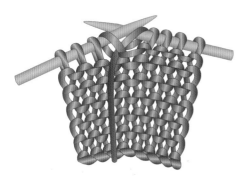

2. Pull the right needle back out through the stitch on the left needle, pulling the wrapped yarn out with it.

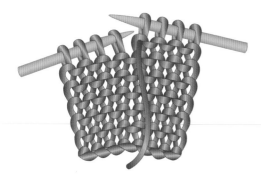

3. As you pull the needle and yarn through, slip the stitch off the left needle.

Repeat these three steps as many times as indicated in the pattern, or until you have transferred all the stitches from the left needle to the right.

BINDING OFF (BO)

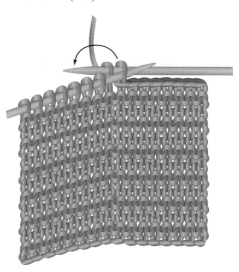

Most of the three-dimensional pieces in this book end with instructions to draw a loose end of yarn through the stitches to close off. For flat pieces, however, the usual finishing technique is to bind off stitches.

Knit the first 2 stitches in the row as you normally would. Slip the left needle into the first stitch you knit, and pull it over the second stitch and completely off the right needle. One stitch is bound off.

Knit the next stitch in the row, so that you again have 2 stitches on the right needle and repeat until there are no more stitches on the left needle and you are left with only one stitch on the right needle.

To finish off, break the yarn, slip the stitch off the needle, and slip the loose end through the stitch. Pull tightly to secure.

NOTE: If a pattern calls for you to bind off on the purl side of a piece, you will bind off in the same way as described above, except that you will purl all stitches instead of knitting them.

INCREASE & DECREASE STITCHES

You need increase and decrease stitches to knit more than a rectangle or a straight tube—like some curves! Although k2tog is the decrease that I use the most often, there are others that come in handy for decreasing by more than one stitch or for a different look.

KNIT THROUGH FRONT AND BACK OF A STITCH (KFB)

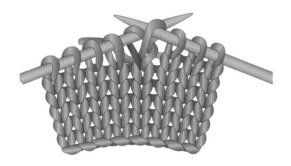

1. Knit a stitch just as you normally would, but without pulling the stitch off the left needle.

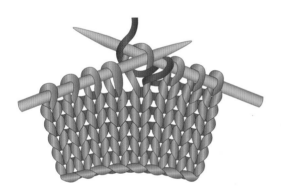

2. Knit into the same stitch again, this time inserting the tip of the right needle through the back leg of the stitch. Once you pull the right needle and yarn through, slip the left stitch off the needle.

This will increase the total number of stitches by 1.

KNIT 2 TOGETHER (K2TOG)

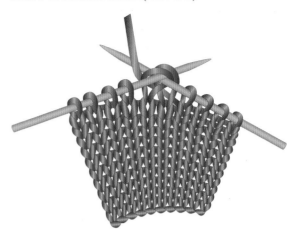

Insert the right needle under the first 2 stitches on the left needle. Wrap the yarn as you would normally do for a knit stitch, and slip both stitches off the left needle.

This will decrease the total number of stitches by 1.

PURL 2 TOGETHER (P2TOG)

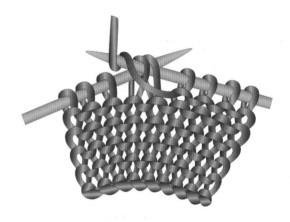

Insert the tip of the right needle purlwise through the front of the first 2 stitches on the left needle. Wrap the yarn around, pull it through, and slip both stitches off the left needle.

This will decrease the total number of stitches by 1.

SLIP, SLIP, KNIT TOGETHER (SSK)

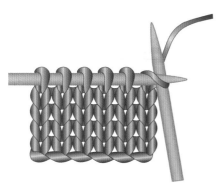

1. Insert the tip of the right needle through the front of a stitch as if to knit, then slip the stitch off the left needle without knitting.

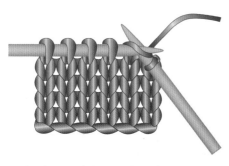

2. Repeat for the next stitch on the left needle.

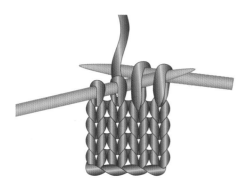

3. Insert the left needle through the front of both slipped stitches on the right needle, and knit together.

This will decrease the total number of stitches by 1.

BEYOND THE BASICS

These additional techniques will help you create the creatures in this book.

BACKWARD LOOP CAST-ON

This is an alternative cast-on technique that gives you a less bulky starting edge. It can also be used in the middle of a piece to add additional stitches.

1. Hold the needle in your right hand. Hold the end of the yarn attached to the ball in your left hand, and loop it around your thumb.

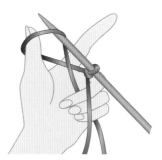

2. Insert the tip of the needle under the yarn on the outside of your thumb.

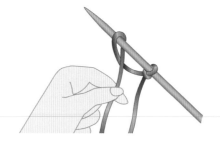

3. Let the yarn on your thumb slip off, and tighten the stitch by pulling gently on it.

Repeat Steps 1–3 until you have cast on the specified number of stitches.

PROVISIONAL CAST-ON

A provisional cast-on, made with a crochet hook, will allow you to go back to your first row of stitches and knit them in the opposite direction. Use waste yarn of a similar weight but a different color from your knitting yarn.

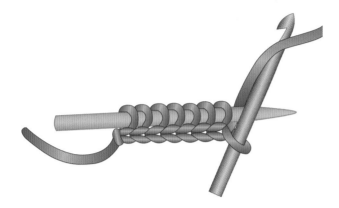

Make a slip knot and place it on the crochet hook. With the hook in your right hand and the knitting needle in your left, bring the yarn behind the needle and to the front above it. Catch the yarn with the hook and pull through to form a chain—you have made one stitch. Repeat until you have the number of stitches called for on the needle, then continue to make a few more chain stitches using the crochet hook only. Cut the waste yarn and gently pull through the last loop in the chain to secure.

Later in the pattern, you will undo the waste yarn so that you can knit from the other direction.

With the piece held right side up, with the waste yarn at the bottom, undo the knot in the waste yarn on the right side, and gently pull the waste yarn to undo it. As the stitches come out, slip a needle under each one to catch it.

KNITTING WITH A CIRCULAR NEEDLE

A circular needle is typically used when knitting in the round with a large number of stitches.

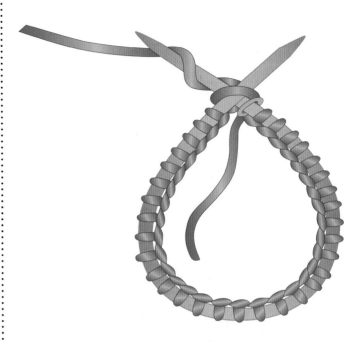

After casting on the stitches, hold the needle with the yarn attached to the stitch on the right. Align the cast-on edge to the inside of the needle—this is important to ensure that you won't twist the stitches.

Place a stitch marker on the right end of the needle. Bring the two ends of the needle close together, and use the right end of the needle to knit the first stitch on the left end of the needle, pulling the yarn from the stitch on the right end to join the two ends together.

Continue to knit from the left end to the right, shifting the stitches around the needle as you go. When you reach the tail end from the cast-on, you have finished knitting one round. Continue to knit the following rounds, resulting in a tube of knitting.

I-CORD

An I-cord is a tiny tube of circular knitting made using two double-pointed needles.

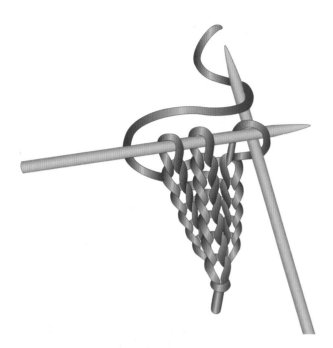

Slide the stitches down the needle in your left hand so that the stitch without the yarn attached is on the right side. Knit the first stitch with the yarn that is connected to the last stitch, pulling the yarn around the back of the needle. Continue to knit to the end of the row.

When you reach the end of the row, instead of turning to work on the other side, again slide the stitches down the needle and knit the first stitch with the yarn that is connected to the last stitch.

YARN OVER (YO)

Yarn over is an increase stitch that makes a small hole in your knitting.

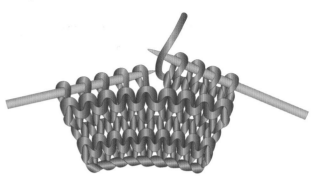

1. Bring the yarn around in front of the needle in your right hand.

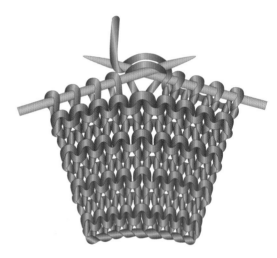

2. Knit the following stitch as you normally would, wrapping the yarn around the needle in the back.

PICKING UP STITCHES ON A FLAT PIECE

Picking up stitches along the side of a finished piece will allow you to knit in another direction and, in the case of toy knitting, it will help you to add another dimension to your knitting. (Some toy patterns call for stitches to be picked up in the middle of a three-dimensional piece. See page 30 for this technique.)

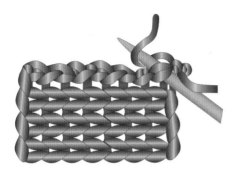

With the piece turned sideways, insert the tip of the needle under the first side stitch. Wrap the yarn around as you would for a knit stitch, and pull the yarn out through the stitch.

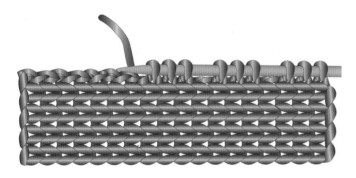

Repeat across the side of the piece, adjusting for the difference between the number of side stitches and the number of stitches to be picked up by skipping every fourth or fifth side stitch.

JOINING A NEW COLOR

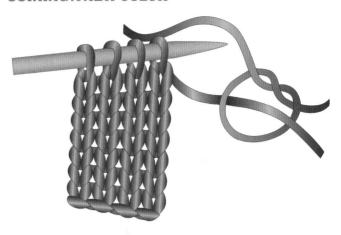

To join a new color of yarn, tie the end of the working yarn and the beginning of the new color yarn together in a loose knot. Knit one stitch with the new yarn, then gently pull the knot tighter and closer to the back or the wrong side of the piece.

Use this technique when a pattern calls for you to switch to a new yarn color and if you won't be using the first color again (or not again for many rows).

As a no-knot alternative, you can twist the tail end of the old color once over the new color yarn after knitting the first stitch in the new color. Then after knitting one row or round with the new color, pull the two tail ends tightly.

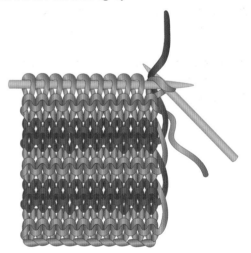

If you will use the first color again soon, as in a striped piece of alternating colors, do not cut the yarn; instead, carry the first color loosely up the side or back of the piece until you will use it again.

STRANDED COLOR KNITTING

Stranded color knitting (or Fair Isle, as it's also known) is a method of carrying multiple strands of different colors of yarn along the back of a piece as you knit, incorporating the different colors in your stitches as you need them. Often there will be a chart to refer to for the color changes.

You want to keep a consistent, relatively loose gauge, without pulling any stitches too tight, so that the finished piece doesn't pucker.

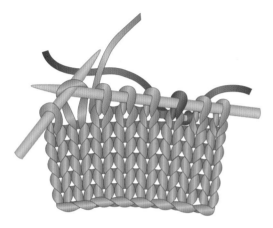

As you knit, you can either hold the two strands of color in different hands or you can simply drop the color that you're not working with at the moment (my preferred method). Wrap the colors of yarn around each other every few stitches to secure the yarn not being used.

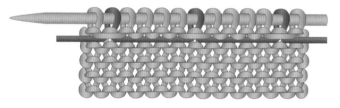

Looking at the back of the piece, you should see the two strands of yarn, smooth and not puckered, across the entire length of a row.

KITCHENER STITCH

The Kitchener stitch allows you to seam two pieces or sections of knitting together in an invisible way.

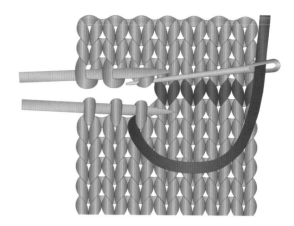

Divide the live stitches onto two needles, with an even number of stitches on each needle. Hold the needles parallel to each other with the working yarn attached to the rightmost stitch on the needle in back.

Cut the working yarn, leaving a long tail, and thread the tail onto a tapestry needle. Insert the tapestry needle purlwise (as if to purl) through the first (rightmost) stitch on the front needle, without slipping the stitch off the needle. Pull the tail through. Next, insert the tapestry needle knitwise through the first stitch on the back needle and pull it through, again without slipping the stitch off the needle. These two stitches set you up to begin the Kitchener stitch pattern.

Now you will repeat the following pattern to finish off the seaming: knit, purl, purl, knit. Insert the tapestry needle knitwise through the first stitch on the front needle, and slip the stitch off the needle. Next, insert the tapestry needle purlwise through the following stitch on the front needle, without slipping the stitch off the needle.

Insert the tapestry needle purlwise through the first stitch on the back needle and slip the stitch off the needle. Then insert the tapestry needle knitwise through the following stitch on the back needle, without slipping the stitch off the needle.

Repeat these four stitches, two front and two back, until only one stitch remains on each needle. Insert the tapestry needle knitwise through the stitch on the front needle and slip it off, then insert the tapestry needle purlwise through the back needle and slip it off.

THREE-NEEDLE BIND-OFF

The three-needle bind-off is a technique with results similar to the Kitchener stitch, but the three-needle bind-off is simpler and is a rougher-looking finish.

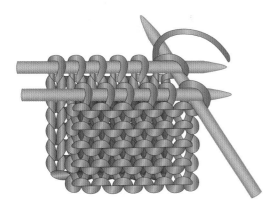

Divide the live stitches onto two needles, with an even number of stitches on each needle. Hold the needles parallel to each other, with the working yarn attached to the rightmost stitch on the needle in back.

Knit the first stitch on the front needle and the first stitch on the back needle together, just like the k2tog technique, except with the stitches running front-to-back instead of side-to-side.

Repeat with the second stitches on each needle.

Now that you have 2 stitches on the needle in your right hand, slip the first (rightmost) stitch over the second stitch, binding off the first stitch.

Next, knit the third pair of stitches together and slip the rightmost stitch on the right needle over the second stitch.

Continue this pattern, knitting two stitches together and then binding off a stitch on the right needle, until there is only the one stitch remaining. To finish off, break the yarn, slip the stitch off the needle and slip the loose end through the stitch. Pull tightly to secure.

PICKING UP A DROPPED STITCH

Dropped stitches happen to the best of us. If you notice that your stitch count is off, you may have a "run" in your knitting, where one stitch has fallen off the needle and a vertical row of stitches has unraveled along with it.

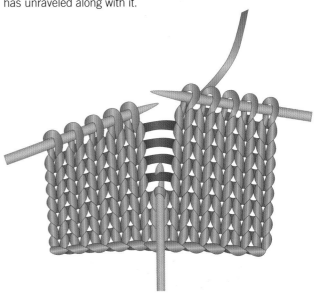

Instead of ripping out the entire piece and starting over, insert a crochet hook through the bottommost stitch that is still in place, then hook the bar that lies directly above it. Pull the bar through the stitch, then repeat for every bar above until you reach your topmost row of stitches.

KNITTING ABBREVIATIONS

Here is a list of abbreviations used in the patterns in this book.

[ ]	Repeat actions in brackets as many times as specified
approx	Approximately
BO	Bind off
CO	Cast on
DPNs	Double-pointed needles
k	Knit
k2tog	Knit 2 stitches together
k3tog	Knit 3 stitches together
kfb	Knit through front and back of one stitch
p	Purl
p2tog	Purl 2 stitches together
pm	Place marker
rnd(s)	Round(s)
RS	Right side
sm	Slip marker
st(s)	Stitch(es)
St st	Stockinette stitch (knit on right side, purl on wrong side)
ssk	Slip 2 stitches onto right needle and then knit them together
WS	Wrong side
yo	Yarn over

RESOURCES

MATERIALS

Yarn

You can use virtually any kind of yarn to create the toys in this book. Go to your local craft or yarn shop to get inspired by the many different options available.

The brand that I used to make the samples in this book, Cascade, comes in a wide variety of fibers, weights, and colors.

CASCADE YARNS
www.cascadeyarns.com

Stuffing

Stuffing can be found in craft stores large and small. Here are some major retailers that carry it.

DICK BLICK ART MATERIALS
www.dickblick.com

HOBBY LOBBY
www.hobbylobby.com

JO-ANN FABRICS AND CRAFTS
www.joann.com

MICHAELS
www.michaels.com

Eyes

Plastic safety eyes can be hard to find in stores, but here are two online sellers with good selections.

HARVEY'S HOBBY HUT
www.harveyshobbyhut.com

6060
www.etsy.com/shop/6060

ONLINE

There are a myriad of knitting tutorials, patterns, and communities online. Here are some of my favorite knitting-related websites.

CRAFTSY
www.craftsy.com
Virtual community and video classes on all types of crafts.

ETSY
www.etsy.com
Marketplace of craftspeople who sell their original handmade crafts, patterns, and vintage goods online.

KNITTING HELP
www.knittinghelp.com
Website with videos demonstrating basic and advanced knitting techniques.

KNITTY
www.knitty.com
Online knitting magazine with lots of fun patterns, including toys.

MOCHIMOCHI LAND
www.mochimochiland.com
My website! You can find many more knitted toy patterns here.

RAVELRY
www.ravelry.com
An online knitting community and a great resource for patterns, yarns, and technical help.

INDEX